Hermit Crab

Hermit Crab

Audrey Pavia

Howell
Book House™

Library of Congress Cataloging-in-Publication Data:

Pavia, Audrey.
    Hermit crab / Audrey Pavia.
        p. cm. — (Your happy healthy pet)
    ISBN-13: 978-0-471-79379-3 (cloth : alk. paper)
    ISBN-10: 0-471-79379-5 (alk. paper)
    1.   Hermit crabs as pets.   I. Title. II. Series.
    SF459.H47P38   2006
    639.67—dc22

                                                                    2006003802

Printed in the United States of America

10   9   8   7   6   5   4   3   2

Book design by Melissa Auciello-Brogan
Cover design by Michael J. Freeland
Book production by Wiley Publishing, Inc. Composition Services

About the Author

Award-winning author **Audrey Pavia** has been a professional pet writer since 1987. A graduate of New York University, Pavia has written 17 books about pet care, including *Horses For Dummies, The Gecko: An Owner's Guide to a Happy Healthy Pet,* and *Guinea Pig: Your Happy Healthy Pet.* She has also written hundreds of articles for pet magazines, including *Reptiles, Aquarium Fish,* and *Critters USA.*

In addition to writing about pets, Pavia has worked as an editor for several dog magazines and a monthly horse publication. She lives with her husband, Randy, and an assortment of animals in Norco, California.

About Howell Book House

Since 1961, Howell Book House has been America's premier publisher of pet books. We're dedicated to companion animals and the people who love them, and our books reflect that commitment. Our stable of authors—training experts, veterinarians, breeders, and other authorities—is second to none. And we've won more Maxwell Awards from the Dog Writers Association of America than any other publisher.

As we head toward the half-century mark, we're more committed than ever to providing new and innovative books, along with the classics our readers have grown to love. This year, we're launching several exciting new initiatives, including redesigning the Howell Book House logo and revamping our biggest pet series, Your Happy Healthy Pet™, with bold new covers and updated content. From bringing home a new puppy to competing in advanced equestrian events, Howell has the titles that keep animal lovers coming back again and again.

Contents

Part I: The World of Hermit Crabs   **10**

Chapter 1: What Is a Hermit Crab?   **13**
Scientifically Speaking   13
Hermit Crab Anatomy   *15*
Mobile Home   16
Hermit Crab Society   17
All Kinds of Crabs   18

Chapter 2: The History of Hermit Crabs   **23**
Prehistoric Crabs   23
Humans and Hermit Crabs   24
The Future of Hermit Crabs   25

Chapter 3: Why Get a Hermit Crab?   **28**
The Joys of Owning a Hermit Crab   28
Your Responsibilities   29
The Cuddle Factor   32
Routine Hermit Crab Care   *33*
Hermit Crabs and Children   34

Chapter 4: Choosing Your Hermit Crabs   **37**
Where to Buy Your Crabs   37
Picking Your Crabs   39

Part II: Caring for Your Hermit Crabs   **44**

Chapter 5: A Home for Your Hermit Crabs   **46**
Establishing the Crabitat   46
Crabitat Accessories   53
Location   58
Acclimating the Newcomers   59
Introducing Other Pets   60

Chapter 6: Feeding Your Hermit Crabs   **61**
What Crabs Eat   61
Great Foods for Your Hermit Crabs   *64*
Recipes for Hermit Crabs   *68*
Serving the Food   69
Water   70

Chapter 7: Your Hermit Crab's Shell   **72**
     Selecting Shells   72
     Shells for Your Crabs   75
     Avoiding Shell Fights   78
     Keeping Shells Wet   79

Chapter 8: Keeping Your Hermit Crabs Healthy   **80**
     Prevention Is Everything   80
     Signs of a Sick Crab   *81*
     Crab Troubles   81
     What Healthy Crabs Need   *88*
     Molting   91

Part III: Enjoying Your Hermit Crabs   **96**

Chapter 9: Hermit Crab Behavior   **98**
     Socializing   98
     Eating   99
     Self-Grooming   99
     Climbing   100
     Digging   101
     Aggression   102
     Crab Sounds   103
     Hiding   103
     Shell Swapping   105

Chapter 10: Having Fun with Your Hermit Crabs   **106**
     Handling   106
     Hand Feeding   108
     Playtime   109
     Traveling with Your Crabs   111
     Meeting Other Crab Owners   114

Appendix: Learning More About Your Hermit Crabs   **116**
     Some Good Books   116
     Education   117
     Online Resources   117

Index   **121**

Shopping List

You'll need to do a bit of stocking up before you bring your hermit crab home. Below is a basic list of some must-have supplies. For more detailed information on selecting each item below, consult chapter 5. For specific guidance on what food you'll need, review chapter 6.

- ☐ Tank with secure, partially vented top
- ☐ Two shallow water dishes
- ☐ Substrate
- ☐ Hiding places
- ☐ Climbing places
- ☐ Food dish
- ☐ Commercial crab food
- ☐ Mister

- ☐ Small plastic travel carrier
- ☐ Tank heater
- ☐ Humidity gauge
- ☐ Temperature gauge
- ☐ Natural sea sponge
- ☐ Water conditioners
- ☐ Shells
- ☐ Decorations

There are likely to be a few other items that you're dying to pick up before bringing your hermit crab home. Use the following blanks to note any additional items you'll be shopping for.

- ☐ _____
- ☐ _____
- ☐ _____
- ☐ _____
- ☐ _____
- ☐ _____
- ☐ _____
- ☐ _____
- ☐ _____
- ☐ _____

Pet Sitter's Guide

We can be reached at (__)_____-_____ Cellphone (__)_____-_____

_____

We will return on _____ (date) at _____ (approximate time)

Other individual to contact in case of emergency _____

_____

_____

Number of hermit crabs we have: _____

Care Instructions

In the following sections, let the sitter know what to feed, how much, and when; what tasks need to be performed daily; and what weekly tasks they'll be responsible for.

Morning _____

_____

_____

_____

Evening _____

_____

_____

_____

Other tasks and special instructions _____

_____

_____

_____

_____

_____

_____

Part I
The World of Hermit Crabs

The Hermit Crab

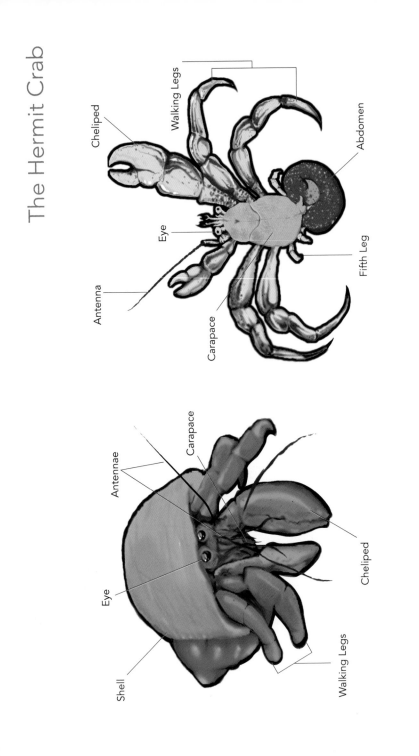

Chapter 1

What Is a Hermit Crab?

Nearly everyone knows what a hermit crab looks like. These charming creatures have been known by humans for centuries. Famous for their ability to inhabit the abandoned shells of other sea creatures, hermit crabs carry their homes around on their backs while prowling seashores and tide pools looking for morsels to eat. Wild hermit crabs have long been the subject of documentaries and cartoons, and are among the most beloved of all sea creatures.

Hermit crabs are not only fascinating as a species, they also make wonderful pets. Fun to watch and easy to care for, they are the first pet of choice for many children. They have also won the hearts of adults the world over.

Scientifically Speaking

Hermit crabs are members of the *Arthropoda* phylum, which means they are related to spiders, insects, and lobsters. But unlike these other arthropods, hermit crabs are crustaceans and therefore have two sets of antennae instead of one.

All arthropods have segmented bodies and jointed legs. Their bodies consist of a head, a thorax, and an abdomen. Hermit crabs also have four antennae, two eyes, a large left claw, and a small right claw. In addition to the claws, a total of eight jointed legs can be found on the hermit crab, four on each side of the body. Of those eight legs, only four are actually used for walking.

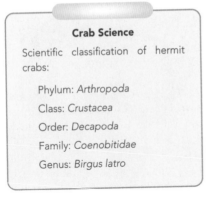

Crab Science

Scientific classification of hermit crabs:

Phylum: *Arthropoda*

Class: *Crustacea*

Order: *Decapoda*

Family: *Coenobitidae*

Genus: *Birgus latro*

A Crustacean

The hermit crab is a crustacean, which means it is part of the same class as shrimp, lobsters, and true crabs. (True crabs have short, hard abdomens, which set them apart from hermit crabs.) Hermit crabs are members of the *Coenobitidae* family, which has two genera: *Coenobita* and *Birgus latro*. *Coenobita* is made up of eleven species of land crab, but the hermit crab is in a genus all his own, *Birgus latro*.

As a crustacean, the hermit crab wears his skeleton on the outside of his body. This exoskeleton is made of areas of thick tissue and softer, more delicate tissue. In the hermit crab, the thick tissue can be found on the animal's claws and torso. The crab's abdomen is covered with the softer exoskeleton, which is why he needs the protection of a "borrowed" shell.

As the hermit crab grows, he must shed his exoskeleton to make room for the new tissue beneath it. This process is called molting.

Hermit crabs who live on land cannot survive underwater. In the wild, they find their food on the ground and in trees.

Hermit Crab Anatomy

The body of the hermit crab is quite different from that of mammals.

- **Abdomen.** The abdominal area of the hermit crab is soft and requires protection from a borrowed shell. The abdomen is slightly curved when outside a shell, but will fold into a tight curve to fit inside a shell home. The digestive and reproductive organs of the crab are located inside his abdomen.
- **Antennae.** The hermit crab has two pairs of antennae that he uses to sense his environment. The antennae are located just below the eyes and consist of one pair of long feelers and one pair of short feelers.
- **Claws.** The hermit crab has two claws, called chelipeds. The left claw is known as the pincher, and is the larger of the two. It is used to close up the opening of the shell when the crab wishes to retreat inside for safety, and for defense. The smaller claw is used mostly for eating and drinking.
- **Eyes.** Hermit crabs have two eyes, which sit at the end of eye stalks that protrude from the front of the head. The stalks can move to enable the crab to see in different directions. The eyes are compound, which means they are made up of many small lenses. The images the crab sees are composed of tiny pieces.
- **Gills.** Although the hermit crab is not a fish, he does have gills on the sides of his body. These gills are usually tucked into the shell and are used for breathing air; hermit crabs cannot breathe underwater. However, the gills must be kept moist to enable the crab to breathe.
- **Legs.** Hermit crabs have four pairs of legs that are used for getting around. Two of these legs protrude from the front of the shell and enable the crab to walk. The back two legs stay inside the shell and help anchor the crab's body.
- **Mouth.** The mouth of the hermit crab is made up of three appendages. The crab uses these appendages to put food into an opening that leads to the digestive system. The appendages work like small hands, helping the crab hold and tear food.

Hermit crabs sometimes lose their legs or eyes in fights and when they are sick or stressed. If the environment is safe and secure and the crab survives the fight or illness, the missing appendage will likely grow back.

Land Creatures

There are land hermit crabs and aquatic ones (see "Aquatic Hermit Crabs" on page 20). Land hermit crabs differ from their aquatic cousins in the obvious way that they live primarily on solid ground. Although they need proximity to the ocean to survive in the wild, hermit crabs will drown if they are kept in an aquatic environment.

Hermit crabs who live on land have small gills but cannot survive underwater. The gills should be kept moist, however, which is one reason it's so important to provide a warm, humid environment for hermit crabs kept in captivity.

Land hermit crabs spend much of their time patrolling their environment for food. In the wild, they feed off the ground and in trees, shoveling food into their mouths using their claws. They are omnivorous scavengers, and their diet consists of decaying plant and animal material. This includes dried leaves, rotten fruit, carcasses, and even feces.

Mobile Home

Hermit crabs are famous for carrying shells around on their backs that don't belong to them. Because the hermit crab has a soft abdomen, he is vulnerable to predators if that part of the body isn't covered. Hermit crabs solve this problem by occupying the shells of gastropods that have died. These may be the shells of sea snails, conches, or other animals. Some hermit crabs have been found wearing fossilized shells from marine creatures that lived eons ago.

Modern hermit crabs who live in the ocean have also taken to using human garbage to house their delicate abdomens. Hermit crabs have been seen wearing bottlenecks, plastic containers, and other discarded items.

Hermit crabs use these shells by tucking their abdomens into the hollow space and then closing up the opening with their pincher claw. They sleep in this position and retreat this way when they feel threatened. When hermit crabs are eating, they extend their heads, their two front claws, and two legs on each side. They amble around using the four extended legs. The four legs that are hidden inside the shell are used to keep the shell in place over the crab's abdomen.

Hermit crabs outgrow their shells as they age and must find new shells to protect their delicate abdomens. Crabs will fight one another for a desirable shell. More aggressive crabs will literally pull weaker crabs out of a shell, and in the wild, will sometimes remove dying gastropods from their shells to gain access.

Hermit crabs find their shells in their environment and switch to bigger ones as they grow.

Hermit Crab Society

Hermit crabs are very sociable creatures, despite their name, and live in groups in the wild. They enjoy being with members of their own species and develop hierarchies within their group. Some crabs are more dominant than others and will show their dominance by pushing each other around.

Hermit crabs also have a voice and will make a chirping sound when the situation warrants it. They use this vocalization with other crabs and sometimes with their humans.

Evening is the most active time for hermit crabs, who prefer to eat and socialize after the sun goes down.

Love Life

In the wild, all hermit crabs breed in the ocean. Male hermit crabs are known for dragging their mates around as they fight off other male crabs who want to mate with their female. When the female begins molting, the male breeds with her and fertilizes the eggs that she carries outside her body.

The female carries 800 to 1,200 fertilized eggs on the outside of her abdomen until they hatch. The young hermit crabs emerge from the eggs just before the full moon of the month after the eggs were fertilized, and only come out of their eggs when the female crab is submerged in seawater.

The baby crabs, known as larvae, must mature through several stages over a period of about two months. They start out as free-swimming creatures and eventually grow into crabs who can walk on the shore.

Hermit crabs have never been bred successfully in captivity, since their eggs will only hatch in the ocean.

All Kinds of Crabs

About 500 hermit crab species can be found in various parts of the world, including the Caribbean, South America, and Australia. Each of these species is unique in appearance, and often in behavior.

Hermit crabs vary in size, from less than an inch to as big as 1 foot. Colors and markings are also varied in the hermit crab world; hermit crabs come in red, brown, purple, and other colors, and sometimes have stripes, spots, or other patterns.

Most Common

The most popular pet hermit crabs are land crabs, which means they live mostly on land near seashores and tide pools. Several species of land hermit crabs are sold in North America. The two most common species sold in pet stores in the United States are from the Caribbean and Ecuador. The Caribbean species is also sold in resort areas in that part of the world.

Because individual hermit crab species are known by many popular names, I have listed them here by their scientific names.

Coenobita clypeatus

The most common land hermit crab available in the United States is *Coenobita clypeatus*. Also known as the West Atlantic land hermit crab, Caribbean land crab, purple pincher crab, purple claw crab, tree crab, and soldier crab, this species can be found in many colors, including purple, red, and brown. They are native to the Bahamas, Belize, Venezuela, the Virgin Islands, the West Indies, and the Florida Keys, and are the species of crab most often sold at beachside stands.

C. clypeatus are nocturnal crabs and hide in leaves or under wet sand during the day to preserve moisture in their shells. Although they prefer living in beach areas, they may stray inland to look for food and search for snail shells. They also climb trees looking for food. *C. clypeatus* prefer to scavenge on the ground,

Coenobita compressus (top) and Coenobita clypeatus (bottom) are the two most common species sold as pets.

however, where they eat dead plants and animals, overripe fruit, and even the feces of other animals.

Coenobita compressus

More commonly known as the Ecuadorian hermit crab, *Coenobita compressus* is the smallest of land hermit crabs. These crabs like salt water even more than other types of land hermit crabs kept in captivity. They enjoy digging and need deep substrate so they can burrow. They are native to the west coasts of North and South America. In the wild, they scour beaches at night looking for food.

Aquatic Hermit Crabs

Land hermit crabs are the most commonly kept hermit crab pets because they are easy to care for. But aquatic hermit crabs can also be kept in captivity—in saltwater aquariums. These crabs may share their home with clown fish, damsel fish, and other tropical marine fish. Because aquatic crabs spend all their lives in the ocean, they fit right in as part of a marine community fish tank.

In the wild, aquatic hermit crabs are found all over the world. They are part of the ocean ecosystem and contribute by scavenging in tide pools, reef shallows, and on the ocean floor.

Aquatic hermit crabs feed on decayed plant matter, algae, and fish food that falls to the bottom of an aquarium. This behavior makes them welcome additions to many aquariums, because they help keep the water clean.

The intertidal hermit crab is another type of crab found in the wild. A member of the *Diogenidae* family, this crab lives in tide pools throughout the world. These crabs require a complex habitat and are not generally kept in captivity.

The pincher claw of *C. compressus* is smaller than that of most other common land hermit crab species, so these crabs prefer shells with narrower openings than those preferred by other species.

C. compressus will live peacefully with other types of hermit crabs, although he prefers living with members of his own species.

Less Common

Hermit crabs that can be found in the United States but are not as common include several species that are native to the African coast and nearby islands.

Coenobita brevimanus

Another hermit crab sometimes found in the pet trade is *Coenobita brevimanus*, commonly referred to as the Indonesian hermit crab. Native to islands on the east coast of Africa and Indonesia, this crab is the largest of the *Coenobita* genus and weighs about half a pound at maturity. In the wild, these crabs get big enough to use coconuts instead of seashells for their homes.

Very social with members of their own species, these crabs enjoy plenty of hiding spaces where they can camp out during the day.

Coenobita cavipes

Sometimes known as the concave hermit crab or the red hermit crab, *Coenobita cavipes* is native to the sandy beaches of eastern Africa. Because these crabs are on the large side, they prefer the abandoned shells of giant African snails.

These very active crabs make good pets. They enjoy climbing and come in a variety of colors.

Coenobita perlatus

Native to Madagascar, *Coenobita perlatus* is also known as the strawberry hermit crab because of its reddish orange colors. These crabs also have white spots on their legs.

These sociable crabs enjoy climbing and visiting with members of their own species. They also love to dig in their substrate.

Where there are tropical beaches, there are hermit crabs.

Coenobita rugosus

These white or gray hermit crabs are native to eastern Africa and the Indo-Pacific region, where they live on sandy beaches and depend on turtle carcasses for much of their diet.

Nicknamed ruggies because of their scientific name, they tend to be a little less active than other land hermit crabs. This species seems to get along well with other crabs and enjoys climbing.

Coenobitidae birgus latro

Also known as the coconut crab or robber crab, *Coenobeitidae birgus latro* is the largest of the hermit crabs. They can grow to weigh as much as 10 pounds and reach 3 feet in diameter. *C. birgus latro* is known as the coconut crab because these big guys can crack coconuts with their pinchers. These crabs also use their claws to climb coconut trees to get at the fruit.

Besides coconuts, this crab eats rotting leaves and other fruit.

C. birgus latro is native to tropical islands in the Pacific and Indian Oceans, and lives in coconut groves and in beach vegetation in the wild. *C. birgus latro* has been known to wander far from the ocean, and has been found in areas as high as several hundred feet above sea level.

C. birgus latro likes to dig in substrate. They come in red or black.

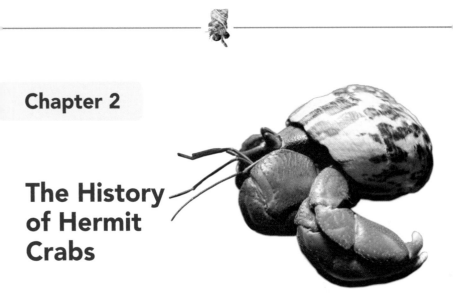

Chapter 2

The History of Hermit Crabs

The hermit crab has an intriguing history, taking us back millions of years. When you look at a hermit crab, you are looking back in time to a period long before there were humans.

Prehistoric Crabs

Hermit crabs are crustaceans, and so share the same early history as shrimp, lobsters, and other shelled sea creatures.

Prehistoric barnacles, which appeared during the Pre-Cambrian period of the Paleozoic Era, are the earliest known crustaceans. The Pre-Cambrian period extends from the birth of our planet to 540 million years ago, making crustaceans among the oldest creatures on Earth.

According to the fossil record, hermit crabs didn't appear until the Cretaceous period, 144 to 65 million years ago. Many hermit crab fossils have been discovered with the crab lying near the shell she inhabited. It is rare for scientists to find a fossil of a hermit crab still in her shell. The reason for this is that many of the hermit crabs who died to create these fossils were slowly buried with sediment at the time of their death. In an effort to climb out of the sediment, the crabs abandoned their shells (originally the shells of the prehistoric arthropod, the ammonite) and began digging to the surface. They died in the process of trying to escape the sand that had enveloped them, leaving behind a fossil record of their struggle.

Other fossil records of hermit crabs include drag traces, which are essentially fossilized footprints of hermit crabs. These drag traces consist of marks in the stone that indicate a hermit crab walked through the sand at that spot.

Fossils of hermit crabs look very much like today's hermit crabs. It's safe to say that hermit crabs have hardly changed at all since prehistoric times.

Humans and Hermit Crabs

We don't know exactly when human beings first started keeping hermit crabs as pets, but it probably started a long time ago. Hermit crabs are easy to capture in the wild and are easy to keep in captivity, so it stands to reason that people in beach areas have been taking these animals home as pets for many, many years.

Hermit Crab Mythology

Because hermit crabs have been around so long, and because they are such fascinating creatures, it's not surprising that these endearing creatures have found their way into the mythology of various cultures over the centuries.

The ancient Greeks, for example, believed in a sea goddess named Skylla who had the upper body of a woman, the tail of fish, and six shark heads around her waist. Homer wrote about Skylla, a monster who prayed on passing sailors, in the *Odyssey*. She was believed to be the goddess of hermit crabs, whose Greek name is *skyllaroi*.

In North America, the Nootka peoples of the Pacific Northwest have a god named Tihtipihin who was the father of all hermit crabs. Tihtipihin and his brother, Kwatyat, allowed themselves to be swallowed by a monster so they could rescue their mother, who had also been swallowed. Once inside the monster, they cut through the monster's stomach and helped their mother to escape.

Hermit crabs have been living on the island of Guam for thousands of years, and, according to legend, Guamanians have developed a way to communicate with them. They claim that by standing in front of the crab, looking her in the eyes, and saying "duk-duk-duk-duk-duk" (*duk* is the name for hermit crab in Chamoru, the native language of Guam), you can get the crab to leave the safety of her shell.

Hermit crabs have been the stuff of legend for centuries, and they still make the news in modern times. Stories of hermit crabs who fled to high ground well before the Asian tsunami of 2004 struck abound in Thailand and other areas where the giant waves hit. Given the hermit crab's deep connection to the sea, it's not hard to believe that these primitive creatures sensed the deadly waves coming.

Hermit crabs are ancient animals, perfectly adapted to the environments in which they live.

Celebrity Crabs

Hermit crabs have long been a favorite of children, who are fascinated by the behavior of these shell-swapping creatures. As a result, there is no shortage of books and cartoons about hermit crabs.

Children's book authors find hermit crabs to be irresistible subjects for adventure. Writer Andrea Weathers made a hermit crab the subject of her book, *Hermy the Hermit Crab Goes Shopping*, which tells the tale of an adventurous hermit crab from South Carolina. *Hector the Hermit Crab,* by Katie Boyce, is another children's book that highlights the growing pains of a shy hermit crab.

In the Disney film *The Little Mermaid*, children around the globe fell in love with Sebastian, the crab who served as King Triton's court composer and conductor.

Television's wildly popular *SpongeBob SquarePants* cartoon also has a crab in a prominent role. Named Mr. Krabs, this whimsical crab is the owner of The Krusty Krab, the fast-food restaurant that employs SpongeBob.

The Future of Hermit Crabs

Like many creatures that inhabit the sea and its surroundings, wild hermit crabs are suffering from human influence on their environment. Many tropical locales that are home to land hermit crabs are experiencing the destruction of seashore habitat. Mangroves, which provide food and shelter to hermit crabs, are being cleared in vast numbers to make room for seaside hotels and condominiums. This leaves the hermit crabs in these areas with nowhere to live.

Some areas where hermit crabs live have so much beach traffic that the crabs are finding a shortage of empty shells to inhabit. Shell collectors gather up the empty shells they find in tide pools and along the beach, leaving the hermit crabs without enough potential homes.

Another threat to hermit crabs in the wild comes from overcollecting. Since hermit crabs do not breed in captivity, all hermit crabs sold in pet stores and through other sources are harvested from the wild. If crabs are gathered faster than they can reproduce, the population of crabs in a given area will suffer. (Unfortunately, many of the crabs who are captured and sold into captivity end up dying soon after because their new owners don't know how to take care of them.)

In some parts of the world, hermit crabs are collected for food. Native peoples who rely on the sea for their sustenance often include hermit crabs in their diet. If they are overcollected, hermit crabs are not able to repopulate themselves and can disappear from places they have inhabited for millions of years.

Shell collectors present a threat to the survival of wild hermit crabs, who may have a hard time finding empty shells for new homes.

Crabs for Sale

If you have ever visited one of the Caribbean islands, especially those off the East Coast of the United States, you have probably seen hermit crabs being sold to tourists from beachside stands. Touted as a living souvenir of the tropics, these hermit crabs were harvested from the wild.

Hermit crabs are also sold in other seaside areas outside the tropics, as well as from kiosks in shopping malls. Pet stores carry them too, of course, and people can even buy hermit crabs on the Internet. The crabs you see for sale from these sources were all imported from tropical locales.

The final threat to hermit crabs is the pollution of coastal waterways. Hermit crabs suffer when pesticides and other waste is dumped into the ocean. Water pollution can devastate the hermit crab population in a small area, leaving that section of the seashore devoid of hermit crabs.

Protecting the ocean and seashore environment, as well as practicing conservative collection measures, are the best ways to help hermit crabs in the wild.

Chapter 3

Why Get a Hermit Crab?

Hermit crabs are popular pets, and it's no wonder. So much fun and enjoyment is available to those who share their homes with these special creatures.

Hermit crabs have a lot to offer both children and adults. There are some great reasons to own hermit crabs.

The Joys of Owning a Hermit Crab

Hermit crabs are intriguing to look at, for several reasons. First are their bodies. Hermit crabs haven't changed much since prehistoric times, so a quick study of their unique bodies gives us a glimpse into eons past.

The shells that hermit crabs carry around on their backs are another part of the visual appeal of these animals. Whether wearing a beautiful natural shell left behind by a conch, or adorned with a specially painted shell with bright colors or elaborate patterns, hermit crabs are fun to look at.

In addition to being pretty, hermit crabs are also fun to observe. They demonstrate a number of interesting behaviors, such as eating, changing shells, exploring their environment with their very active antennae, climbing, and digging.

A healthy hermit crab, when not sleeping, is always on the go. Watching these animals interact with their tankmates is another enjoyable part of crab ownership.

Ease of Care

Hermit crabs are one of the easiest pets to take care of, and can live to a ripe old age of 10 if you just give them the basic ingredients they need for life.

An aquarium with the proper substrate, a heater, food and water dishes, and hiding and climbing elements are all your crabs need for a happy life.

Crabs require daily feedings and fresh water, and you'll need to clean up their waste and uneaten food each day. These tasks, along with monitoring the heat and humidity levels in their crabitat, are all you need to do to care for your hermit crabs.

Inexpensive

Hermit crabs are inexpensive pets to purchase and maintain. Your primary costs will come with setting up the tank, but after these items have been purchased, all you need are the crabs. Small hermit crabs are usually priced under five dollars each, and larger crabs aren't much more.

Your crabs will need regular substrate changes, and daily food and water. The cost for these items is negligible, making hermit crabs one of the most affordable pets available today.

Your Responsibilities

Pet ownership is a big commitment, even if the pet you are considering is a little hermit crab. Compared to a dog, cat, or bird, a hermit crab is easy to care for. Hermit crabs don't need to go on walks or be trained. As a hermit crab owner, you can leave your pet alone for hours or even days, if you provide enough food and water to last during that time. Hermit crabs don't need to see the vet for shots every year, either. They are also much easier to clean up after than your average dog, cat, or bird.

That doesn't mean hermit crabs are maintenance-free, though. Hermit crabs have important requirements that must be met, or they will die a premature death. You will be responsible for the life of this creature, so it's important to examine your situation to make certain you are ready to take on the role of caretaker.

Daily Attention

Before you go out and buy two or more hermit crabs (hermit crabs should never live alone), make sure crab ownership is really right for you. Consider your lifestyle first and figure out if you have the time and inclination to provide the care your crabs will need. Consider whether your job, school, or other commitments will allow you to set aside time every day to care for your crabs.

Do You Have Space?

Another point to consider when making your decision about whether to share your home with hermit crabs is space. Do you have enough room in your home for the appropriate size terrarium for the type and number of crabs you intend to keep? Don't shortchange your crabs because you want to economize on space. The more room crabs have to live, the better off they will be.

Cost

Another consideration when thinking about crab ownership is cost. The price of the crabs and their setup will be your primary financial commitment. The whole package could run you as much as $100 or more, depending on factors such as the size of the setup, the number of crabs you buy, and the equipment you choose.

On the positive side, once your crabs are set up in their new home, the amount of money you will have to spend on food, substrate, and other accessories will be negligible.

Hermit crabs need daily care and a relatively complex habitat. You must be ready to supply these things for your crab.

cleaning up the uneaten food and other debris in the cage. It's important for parents to supervise these tasks, however, to make sure the crabs are receiving proper care.

If you are buying hermit crabs for your kids, think before you buy. Consider whether your kids are old enough to learn to respect the crabs and admire them from afar. Hermit crabs should not be handled by very young children. A hermit crab can easily fall from his shell if not properly handled, and can be seriously hurt in a fall. Hermit crabs who are afraid of being handled or of falling will use their claws to administer a pinch. They will no doubt upset your child, and possibly cause him or her to drop the crab.

Very young children cannot be expected to understand that a hermit crab should not be touched. If you can't find a way to keep the crabs out of the reach of a small child, consider waiting until your kids are older.

If you have older children, you don't have to worry too much about problems with handling. However, you do have to worry about taking on the responsibility

Children can be given some responsibility for hermit crab care, but an adult should always supervise and make sure the crabs are receiving the best possible care.

of caring for the crabs. Despite promises that they will care for the pet themselves, most kids don't follow through every time. Although they have the best of intentions, most children do not have the attention span required for the care of hermit crabs—or any pet.

If you decide to allow your child some responsibility in caring for the crabs, make sure you are there to monitor the pets' well-being. No child should be given unsupervised responsibility for any animal. Children cannot be expected to recognize signs of illness, or to be able to judge the crabs' general health. An adult should always be a pet's primary caregiver. Any other arrangement could result in harm to the crabs, either through neglect or inexperience on the part of the child. And when your child eventually loses interest, as most kids do, it will be your responsibility to take over completely.

Chapter 4

Choosing Your Hermit Crabs

Hermit crabs are charming and fascinating creatures. Any animal who carries her house around on her back warrants attention! But before you go out and buy hermit crabs, you need to think about a few things.

Where to Buy Your Crabs

You will probably have to buy your hermit crab, mostly like at a pet shop. If you are visiting a Caribbean island, you may even see hermit crabs for sale on the street.

If the idea of so many hermit crabs being taken from the wild makes you uneasy, you can call around to animal shelters, which occasionally have hermit crabs available. If you know someone who wants to give away a hermit crab because the person can no longer take care of her, you may end up adopting one. Or you may know of an animal rescue group in your area that is trying to find a home for a hermit crab. These situations are rare, though. In most cases, if you want hermit crabs in your life, you will have to buy them.

Pet Stores

A good place to buy hermit crabs is a retail pet store that specializes in reptiles and invertebrates. These stores usually employ people who are skilled at caring for exotic animals such as crabs. The hermit crabs who have been imported to be sold through these shops have usually been acclimated to captivity, and therefore tend to be healthy.

You can also buy your hermit crabs from a reliable pet store that sells reptile and aquarium fish supplies. Make sure the hermit crabs look well cared for and that the store offers a health guarantee on its crabs.

Internet Sellers

A growing number of Internet retailers are offering hermit crabs for sale. If you buy a crab through one of these sources, you order the crab online and have it shipped to you. Although you can get good crabs from many of these sources, you are at a disadvantage shopping this way because you can't examine the crab before making your purchase. Also, the shipping is stressful for the crab.

Reputable sellers guarantee the crab's health, so if the animal arrives dead or dies soon after you receive her, you should be able to get a refund or a replacement crab. If you'd rather not deal with this possibility, buy a crab from a local retailer instead.

Stands and Kiosks

Hermit crabs are often sold from boardwalk stands in resort areas and from shopping mall kiosks. Buying a crab from one of these sources can be risky, because the crab is probably stressed from lack of proper care (many are kept in fish bowls or small plastic or wire cages), and may die not long after you take her

Try not to get just one. Hermit crabs are very special animals and will enjoy living in groups.

> ### The More, the Merrier
>
> Because hermit crabs are such sociable creatures in the wild, it's important to get more than just one crab. Two is the minimum number you should keep, but three or more is even better.
>
> The more crabs you have, the larger your setup will need to be, however, so think about the size of tank you can accommodate before you purchase your crabs. A 10-gallon tank can safely accommodate a maximum of six crabs who are less than 2 inches long. If the crabs grow larger, you'll need to move them to a 20-gallon tank for their comfort.

home. You may have little recourse for getting your money back under these circumstances, since the vendor may not be around for very long.

Adoption

Some crabs are available for free, either from private owners who wish to find new homes for their crabs, or as prizes at carnivals or other contests. If you rescue a crab from an unpleasant situation, you'll be doing a good deed. Just be sure the crab is healthy before you take her home. Once a crab becomes seriously ill, it's unlikely you'll be able to save her.

If you want to adopt a crab in need, check with your local animal shelter. On occasion, hermit crabs are surrendered to animal shelters when people no longer want them.

You can also contact reptile rescue groups in your area to find out if they are trying to find homes for any hermit crabs. (Even though hermit crabs are not reptiles, some reptile rescue groups will take them.) To find a reptile rescue group in your area, search the Internet or call veterinarians in your area who advertise that they treat exotic pets. Such vets may be aware of reptile rescue groups near your home.

Picking Your Crabs

Now that you know where to go to buy your hermit crabs, what should you look for when you are picking out your pets?

Species

The two varieties of hermit crabs most often seen in pet shops in North America are the Caribbean land crab *(Coenobita clypeatus)* and the Ecuadorian hermit crab *(Coenobita compressus)*. Sometimes labeled as small and medium crabs, or even jumbo crabs, these two species basically require the same care, with the exception that *C. compressus* needs a little less salt in the water. Find out which species you are buying so you know how to take proper care of your pets.

Health

It's important to start out right by selecting crabs who are in good health. You can tell a healthy hermit crab by counting to make sure all four of the legs that protrude from the shell are visible, along with the two claws. Crabs who are stressed tend to lose their limbs and are at a disadvantage, healthwise. Also, crabs who show more than four legs are in a shell that is too small and are probably stressed.

Take a look at the crab's head and what you can see of her body to make sure there is no visible damage, such as abrasions or holes. If the crab is housed with a lot of other crabs, she may have fallen victim to a shell fight and could have wounds as a result. These wounds could become infected, resulting in the crab's death not long after you buy her.

The hermit crabs you choose should have all their legs and claws. But crabs who show more than four legs are in a shell that is too small and are probably stressed.

What Sex Is that Crab?

If you have your heart set on one gender or another, you are probably out of luck. The only way to tell the sex of a hermit crab is if the crab is out of her shell, and it's unlikely the crabs you'll see in the pet store or other environment will be out of their shells. Since you can't force a hermit crab out of her shell without harming her, you won't be able to tell for sure whether the crabs you are considering are male or female. Even out of the shell, only true experts can tell the difference.

A hermit crab's reproductive organs are located toward the back of the body, and are usually hidden by the shell. If you are lucky enough to see your crab outside of her shell, or sticking pretty far out of it, you'll have to look quickly to get a look at the reproductive organs. Another way to check is to view the crab's exoskeleton after she molts but before she eats the discarded material.

Unlike most animals, it's easier to see that a particular crab is female. The female crab has organs called genopores on the first segment of the back walking legs. These are tiny, round openings into which the male inserts sperm during mating.

Although it's only possible to determine the gender of a crab if this section of the body is outside the shell, resist the temptation to try to pull the crab from her shell to get a look at her reproductive organs. This is very stressful for the crab, and may result in fatal injury.

Of course, the sex of the crab doesn't really matter, since hermit crabs don't breed in captivity.

Look for crabs who are active, although keep in mind that hermit crabs are nocturnal, so they tend to sleep during the day. If possible, shop for crabs in the evening when they are most likely to be moving around. You can try blowing on the crabs or misting them with water to get them moving. If a crab won't come out of her shell, hold the crab in your hand and try to feel movement inside the shell. If you feel the crab moving around, the animal is probably healthy.

Once the crab comes out of her shell, look for a lot of antennae activity. A healthy hermit crab is always moving her antennae around, exploring her environment.

When you lift up the crab, make sure she has some weight to her. Crabs who feel light may be sick or dehydrated. You may have to pick up several crabs of the same size to get a feeling for how much they should weigh.

Be sure to take notice of the enclosure. Look for a crabitat that is clean and odor-free. Make sure the tank isn't overcrowded with crabs. You'll know there are too many crabs if they are crawling all over each other because they have no choice. Be sure the enclosure is clean, too. A dirty tank puts the crabs at risk for disease.

Examine the crabs for mites and other small bugs. These can be seen crawling around on the substrate and on the crabs, and lurking between the crabs' legs. If you see bugs in the environment or on the crabs, don't buy a crab from that enclosure.

Age and Size

It's not a good idea to keep young crabs with larger, fully grown crabs because the older crabs may pick on the young ones. So try to keep crabs of the same age.

It's not a good idea to keep big crabs and little crabs together in the same enclosure, because the bigger ones are likely to pick on the smaller ones.

If you don't know the age of the crabs you have at home or the ones available in the pet shop, try to keep crabs of the same size. It's never a good idea to mix large crabs with small crabs because the smaller ones are likely to be bullied by the bigger ones. Instead, buy crabs that are all about the same size to avoid fights, or the small ones being eaten by the bigger ones.

Although very tiny crabs may seem cute, it's not a good idea to buy these very small creatures unless you have a lot of experience keeping hermit crabs. Small crabs are usually young and more delicate than their older, larger counterparts. A small crab is more likely to die in her new environment than a larger, older crab is.

Part II

Caring for Your Hermit Crabs

Chapter 5

A Home for Your Hermit Crabs

Before you bring your hermit crabs home, you need to be prepared. Having your new pets' abode and accessories on hand, set up, and ready to go will help your crabs adapt to their new surroundings.

Establishing the Crabitat

If you want your crabs to live long, healthy lives, pay careful attention to how you set up your pets' environment, or crabitat. The right enclosure and surroundings are mandatory if your crabs are to survive in captivity.

The Tank

The first and most important part of your crabs' new home will be the tank they live in—filled with all the accessories they need to be comfortable. Because hermit crabs thrive in warm, humid environments, the best housing for these unique creatures is a glass aquarium with a mostly solid cover. The glass will help keep humidity inside the crabitat (as opposed to plastic or wire enclosures, which will not). Glass will also make the enclosure easy to clean.

The size of the tank will depend on how many crabs you plan to house. The more space you can provide your crabs, the better. They will be happier and healthier if they can move around freely and feel comfortable in their new home. A good general rule is to limit your crabitat to six small crabs per

10-gallon tank. This will leave plenty of room for climbing areas, food and water dishes, and hiding spaces. Anything smaller will prevent the crabs from living a normal life and will shorten their life spans.

If you have room for a larger tank, that's even better. Remember that before your hermit crabs came to live with you, they had unlimited space in which to roam. Provide them with the biggest living area you can manage.

> **WARNING**
>
> Some crabs are sold in goldfish bowls, but these are not adequate permanent homes for hermit crabs. Crabs kept under these circumstances will live only a few months.

Because hermit crabs are such good climbers—and notorious escape artists—you'll want to have a secure lid on your tank to keep your pets safely inside. A top that is mostly solid to help preserve heat and humidity, but with a small screened or vented area for ventilation, is your best choice. Without ventilation, condensation will build up on the inside of the tank and encourage harmful bacterial growth.

This tank has everything a hermit crab needs: dishes, places to climb and hide, soft substrate, heat, humidity, and a cover.

Substrate

Crabs spend much of their time on the floor of their crabitat, as well as digging through it, so it's important to provide them with the right substrate. Small crabs need at least 4 to 5 inches of substrate, while large crabs prefer the substrate to be 7 to 10 inches deep. The substrate should be deep enough that your crab can burrow into it and cover himself.

When you visit your local pet supply store, you'll see several options for hermit crab substrates. Select a material that will be easy to clean and still be healthy and comfortable for your pets. The following section describes some of the more popular options. To keep your crabs healthy and happy, choose one of these substrates for your pets. Do not use wood shavings, paper substrates, or anything specifically designed for use with desert reptiles, since these do not provide the best environment for your crabs.

Sand

Packaged sand designed just for hermit crabs is a popular choice for many hermit crab owners. Sand is a natural substrate for crabs, and the type that is packaged specifically for their use is often high in calcium to help meet the crabs' needs for this important mineral.

Sand makes an attractive substrate and is available in a wide variety of colors, from natural to bright pink. Crabs like to burrow in it and scuttle across it. Sand substrate makes it easy to pick up your crabs' waste. Using a small strainer, you can scoop up the feces and toss it in the trash.

The downside of sand is that it can be messy. Woe if you happen to spill any on your floor. You'll spend a lot of time with the vacuum cleaner trying to pick up every last grain. Sand also clumps when it gets wet, so you may find your crabs crawling over clumps of damp sand, especially near their water dishes.

It's okay to go collect sand from an ocean beach for the crabitat, but it must be cleaned thoroughly before being used for hermit crabs. First rinse the sand under running water until the water runs clear. Then spread it out in shallow pans and dry it in the sun. This is a pretty labor-intensive, messy process, which is why many people prefer to buy the packaged sand at the pet supply store. Also, the packaged sand made for hermit crabs usually has calcium added, which some people think is beneficial for the crabs.

Aquarium Gravel

Pet supply stores sell small, smooth pebbles, designed to be used in fish aquariums, that can also be used as substrate for hermit crabs. The gravel pieces should be very smooth and small enough that your crabs can burrow into the substrate.

Aquarium gravel is not as easy to keep clean as sand, but it is very attractive. Just remember that you will have to wash it regularly.

Gravel isn't as easy to keep clean as sand, and will require regular washing so waste doesn't build up to a harmful level in your crabitat. Gravel makes an attractive substrate, however, and is the choice of many hermit crab owners.

Bark and Mulch

Commercially packaged bark and mulch (sometimes made from coconut fiber) designed for humidity-loving reptiles is also a good choice for your crabitat. These substrates are meant to maintain humidity levels in the terrarium and encourage digging—something hermit crabs love to do.

You can clean soiled areas of bark and mulch by scooping them up with a small strainer or shovel. Unlike gravel substrate, bark and mulch can't be washed, and so it should be completely replaced every few months.

Heat

Hermit crabs are native to warm climates, so it's crucial for your crabs' health that you provide a source of heat in your crabitat. Crabs are unable to generate their own body heat, and are completely dependent on their environment to stay warm.

The temperature in your pets' crabitat should always be between 76 and 82 degrees Fahrenheit. You can achieve this by using heating devices designed specifically for cold-blooded creatures such as hermit crabs.

Undertank Heater

Probably the best way to heat your crabitat is with an undertank heater. Designed to attach to the underside of the tank floor, these heaters send warmth up through the substrate into the crabitat. They cover only a section of the tank's underside, which enables the crabs to move from a warmer part of the tank floor to a cooler part whenever they feel they need a break from the heat. Undertank heaters stay plugged in all the time, providing a constant source of heat for your crabs.

Heat Lamp

Designed for use with reptiles, heat lamps are a second choice for crabitats. These lamps heat the tank from above and provide light to see crab activity at night.

The problem with some heat lamps is that they can provide too much warmth for a small hermit crab habitat, causing stress to the crabs and possible dehydration. If you decide to use a heat lamp, carefully monitor the temperature in your crabs' enclosure to make sure it does not get too warm.

Thermometer

In addition to a heating element, you'll need a thermometer to help you keep track of the temperature in your crabitat. You can buy a terrarium thermometer at your local pet supply store that can be attached to the outside of your tank. Secure it to the upper corner of the tank that is farthest from the heating element, as this will give you a more accurate reading of the tank's overall temperature.

> ### CAUTION
>
> **Other Heaters**
>
> Other heating elements made for reptiles, such as heat rocks and heat emitters, are not good choices for hermit crabs. These devices can overheat your crabitat, making your crabs uncomfortable and possibly dehydrated. Heat rocks are particularly dangerous to hermit crabs, since the crabs can be burned if they try to climb on the rock.

Insulation

If you live in an area with very cold winters, you may find that you have trouble keeping your crabs' enclosure warm enough with just a heating element. You can solve this problem by insulating your crabitat with foam board. Cut the foam board to exactly cover three sides of the tank and secure the board to the outside of the glass using duct tape. The board will provide insulation and your pets' tank will stay warmer. To make it more appealing, you can decorate the foam board or purchase a printed aquarium background to provide an attractive scene for your hermit crabs.

Remember to always monitor the thermometer to make sure the temperature inside your crabitat is between 76 and 82 degrees Fahrenheit. If the temperature goes under 70, take immediate steps to warm up the environment, either by insulating the tank or adding another heater.

If the tank becomes too warm—which can sometimes happen in areas where summers are hot and homes are not air-conditioned—you'll need to cool down the tank by removing insulation or temporarily turning off the heating element.

Humidity

Humidity is almost as crucial as warmth when it comes to hermit crabs, and it's important you keep the air in your crabs' tank humid. Without the proper humidity, your hermit crabs will become ill and eventually die.

Hermit crabs will die without the proper humidity. Add natural sea sponges to your crabs' water dishes to maintain the humidity level in the crabitat.

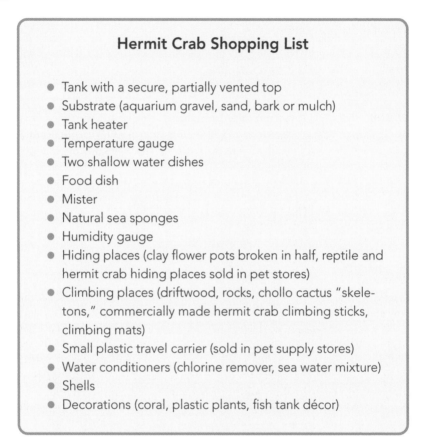

Hermit Crab Shopping List

- Tank with a secure, partially vented top
- Substrate (aquarium gravel, sand, bark or mulch)
- Tank heater
- Temperature gauge
- Two shallow water dishes
- Food dish
- Mister
- Natural sea sponges
- Humidity gauge
- Hiding places (clay flower pots broken in half, reptile and hermit crab hiding places sold in pet stores)
- Climbing places (driftwood, rocks, chollo cactus "skeletons," commercially made hermit crab climbing sticks, climbing mats)
- Small plastic travel carrier (sold in pet supply stores)
- Water conditioners (chlorine remover, sea water mixture)
- Shells
- Decorations (coral, plastic plants, fish tank décor)

Your crabitat needs to be maintained at a relative humidity level of around 60 to 70 percent. This won't be difficult to accomplish if you live in a warm, humid climate year-round. However, if your summers are dry and/or your winters are cold, you'll need to provide a source of humidity for your crabs.

Water Dishes

You'll need to provide at least two water dishes for your crabs to drink from, but you can add a few more to help provide humidity to the environment. Be careful not to place the water dishes over an undertank heating element, as crabs may dig under the dish and get too close to the heater.

Natural Sea Sponges

By adding sea sponges to the water dishes, you'll increase the humidity levels inside the tank. Make sure you buy only natural sea sponges, which are available in pet supply stores. Commercial cleaning sponges are dangerous to your crabs.

Mister

Spraying the sides of your crabs' tank daily with a mist of lukewarm, distilled water will help keep up the humidity levels in your crab's environment.

Humidity Gauge

You'll need a humidity gauge in your crabs' tank to help you keep track of humidity levels. You can buy one at a pet supply store. The gauge should be attached to the inside of the tank, where you can easily read it.

Lighting

The good news about hermit crabs is that you don't need to provide them with any additional lighting other than what they receive naturally in your home.

If you do choose to put a light on them during the day to help illuminate their enclosure and make it easier to see them, use one that is designed for reptiles and provides full-spectrum lighting. These light fixtures do not give off heat, but they do simulate sunshine. Because crabs naturally live outdoors, it can only help them to have artificial sunshine during the daylight hours.

If you use full-spectrum lighting, be sure to turn the light off at night so the crabs know when it's evening.

Crabitat Accessories

Now that you have the main items covered for your hermit crabs' new habitat, you'll need to add some accessories. The following items will help your crabs feel right at home in their new surroundings.

Water Dishes

Hermit crabs need both fresh and salt water in their environment in order to stay healthy. You can provide these sources in two separate shallow water dishes. When choosing your pets' water dishes, make sure they aren't so deep that the crabs can't climb out. Smaller crabs can easily drown in water dishes that are too deep.

Shallow seashells make great food dishes for your hermit crabs, because they can easily climb in and out of them.

The best dishes are the types sold at pet supply stores specifically for reptiles. These dishes have the right shape and depth to give your crabs easy access. They are also designed to have a natural look that will work well in your crabs' environment.

Food Bowl

An important part of your hermit crabs' diet is commercial crab food. You'll need a dish to serve this to your pets. Food dishes made especially for hermit crabs are a good choice, because they have a ramp so the crabs can easily enter and exit the bowl. (Hermit crabs like to sit in their food dish while they eat.)

Clam, oyster, and scallop shells also make good food bowls for hermit crabs. Simply turn them bowl side up and nestle them into the substrate. Your crabs will crawl into the shells to enjoy their meals.

Hiding Places

Hermit crabs are nocturnal, which means they prefer to sleep during the day. They enjoy tucking themselves under little shelters and huddling there until it's time to wake up and socialize.

Pet supply stores carry a variety of shelters designed primarily for reptiles that are also great for hermit crabs. Some stores even have special hermit crab shelters.

Give your crabs plenty of shelters to choose from, and look for different styles. Make sure the entrance to the shelter is high enough to accommodate your crabs' shells.

You can also make your own hermit crab hiding places out of driftwood, hollowed out tree limbs, concave rocks, coconut shells, and other items found in nature. Just be sure that whatever hiding place you choose won't tip over onto your crabs if your pets decide to climb on it.

Your hermit crab will appreciate some cozy hiding places.

Climbing Places

Hermit crabs love to climb, so be sure to provide them with places they can scale. Commercially packaged climbing sticks are available, or you can gather items from nature such as driftwood, textured wood and rocks, and chollo cactus "skeletons."

Another option to satisfy your crabs' climbing instincts is a commercially made climbing mat. Made from natural fibers, these mats attach to the side of a tank and offer traction so the crabs can climb. When misted with water, the mats also help keep the crabitat humid.

TIP

If you opt for a climbing mat, be sure your tank has a very secure lid on it, or your crabs are likely to escape.

Make sure that whatever climbing places you choose are stable and won't tip over when your crabs begin their ascent.

Food

Chapter 6 covers what to feed your hermit crabs. But for your shopping list here, be sure to purchase a supply of top-quality commercial crab food before

In addition to fresh foods, your crabs will need a top-quality commercial crab food.

you bring your crabs home. You can buy crab food at a pet supply store. The other food items your crab will enjoy are probably already in your kitchen.

Water Conditioners

Your hermit crabs need fresh water and salt water to stay healthy. Be sure to purchase a product that will remove the chlorine from fresh water (including bottled water). You should also buy a product that will enable you to make salt water for your pets. Both of these items can be found in pet stores that sell supplies for hermit crabs.

Shells

Although your hermit crabs already have shells, it's a good idea to provide additional shells in their crabitat in case they want to or need to change homes. Buy shells of different sizes and shapes and leave them in your pets' tank. (For more information, see chapter 7, "Your Hermit Crab's Shell.")

Extra shells are especially important if you have a lot of crabs, since you want to avoid potentially deadly shell fights—that is, crabs fighting with each

You can decorate the crabitat any way you like. Aquarium decorations with smooth edges work well, and your crabs will enjoy having lots of places to climb and hide.

other over shells. The more shells available to the crabs, the less likely it is that they will fight.

Decorations

You may want to add some decorative items to your crabs' habitat. Fish tank decorations, plastic plants, and coral all make good decorative accessories for the crabitat. Be aware that your crabs will likely crawl all over whatever you put in their tank, so make sure the items do not have any sharp points or edges.

Travel Carrier

You will find times when you need to remove your hermit crabs from their crabitat and keep them in temporary housing while you transport them or clean out their enclosure. A small plastic travel carrier, available at pet supply stores, will work for this.

Your travel carrier can also work as an enclosure for molting crabs. Some crab owners opt to separate a molting crab from his tankmates for the crab's safety. If you use a plastic travel carrier for this purpose instead of another glass tank, you'll have to mist the enclosure several times a day to keep it moist.

Location

When considering where to locate your crabs' tank, keep in mind that you want your pets to be warm and free of drafts, yet not too close to a heating element. You also want to avoid direct sun, because the tank can quickly overheat.

Avoid damp, dark places for your crabs' enclosure, since they won't do well under such conditions. Instead, put your crabs' tank in a place in your home that is well-lit and comfortable.

Hermit crabs are nocturnal, so consider placing your crabitat in an area where you spend a lot of time in the evening. This might be the living room where you are watching television, or in your child's bedroom where he or she spends time doing homework, playing on the computer, or talking to friends on the phone. This way, your family will have a chance to watch your crabs' antics when the sun goes down.

On the other hand, keep your crabs' enclosure out of your bedroom if you want to sleep at night. Crabs make a lot of noise moving around during the night, and they may keep you awake.

It's a good idea to have a small travel carrier where you can place your crabs when you are cleaning the crabitat or if you must move them. Be cautious with your crabs around other pets.

Adding More Crabs

Hermit crabs can become stressed and ill when they are moving to a new home. Imagine how difficult it must be for a crab to go from living in the wild to suddenly being captured and transported several times before reaching his final destination.

To help your new crab make an easy, gradual transition to this new life, keep him isolated upon arrival for a few days, before you place him in the tank with other crabs.

To isolate your new crab, put him in a separate tank of his own, complete with heater, substrate, water, food, and other items he needs. Allow him to rest in this separate tank until he becomes active and starts to explore. Once he seems comfortable, you can put him in a crabitat with other crabs.

Acclimating the Newcomers

The day you bring your crabs home will be an exciting one. Everyone in your family will be anxious to see and hold the newcomers.

When your pets are placed in their new enclosure, they will likely hide in their shells for awhile, possibly for a couple of days. Your crabs have been through a lot in a short time. They were taken from the wild, shipped to a pet store, and have now been taken to a new home. They are no doubt frightened and uncertain about what is happening to them.

To help minimize stress on your new pets, it's a good idea to let the crabs settle in for a few days before handling them. Keep in mind that your new crabs don't know where they are, and may not even know each other if you purchased them from separate sources. They need time to relax and acclimate to their new environment before they meet your family.

Once your crabs have had a few days to settle in, you can pick them up and hold them (see chapter 10, "Having Fun with Your Hermit Crabs," for more on handling your crabs). Keep visiting sessions short so as not to stress your crabs. Eventually, when they are completely comfortable in their new home, you can spend more time handling them.

Introducing Other Pets

It's unlikely that any of your other pets will have an interest in your hermit crabs. Cats, dogs, and birds take little notice of them. However, that doesn't mean you shouldn't take precautions with your crabs' safety. While your cat or dog may not even know your crabs exist when your new pets are sleeping in their crabitat, a crab who is scuttling across the floor will surely attract the attention of a dog or cat. The end result could be disastrous for your crab.

When you take your crabs out to handle them or let them play on the floor, keep cats and dogs out of the room for the crabs' safety. It's better to be safe than sorry.

Chapter 6

Feeding Your Hermit Crabs

The nutritional needs of hermit crabs are relatively easy to meet. It's important to learn what those needs are, however, if you want your crabs to be happy and healthy. The way you feed your crabs can mean the difference between long-lived pets and sickly animals who die young.

In nature, hermit crabs are both omnivores and scavengers, which means they eat just about anything they can catch or find lying around. This diet gives hermit crabs the greatest chance to obtain a variety of vitamins and minerals from their environments.

It is difficult to provide captive hermit crabs with the kind of variety and nutrition that they would naturally find in the wild. But if you try, you can give your hermit crabs enough food variety to keep them healthy and satisfied.

What Crabs Eat

Because hermit crabs enjoy a smorgasbord of different foods, you have a variety of options when it comes to feeding your pets.

Crab Food

A good commercial crab food should be the staple of your pets' diet. You can buy crab food at a pet supply store or any place that sells hermit crabs. Crab foods are high in protein and contain vitamins and minerals to help ensure crabs get all the nutrients they need.

Commercial crab foods come in a variety of types, including dry pellets, flakes, and cakes. One company even makes canned crab food.

If you feed dry crab food, moisten it with a spray of water before you offer it to your crabs. If the pellets are large and you have small crabs in your crabitat, crush the pellets into a powder so the little crabs can fit the food in their mouths.

Vegetables

Veggies are an important part of your crabs' diet and should be offered daily, chopped in small pieces. Green vegetables can provide calcium to your crabs as well as vitamin A and other essential nutrients. Some green vegetables that crabs enjoy include spinach, chard, kale, bok choy, collard greens, dandelion leaves, romaine lettuce (not iceberg), and broccoli.

Because hermit crabs need carotene in their diet to stay healthy, you should also feed them carrots to help them get this important nutrient.

Organic vegetables are the best type to feed your crabs, because these foods have not been sprayed with pesticides or grown with chemical fertilizers. You can buy organic produce in health food stores and even in some regular markets.

Another option is to grow your own hermit crab vegetable garden. Gardening is a fun hobby, and planting, tending, and harvesting your crabs'

Fresh vegetables are an important part of your crabs' diet. Make sure they have not been sprayed with pesticides.

food can be a lot of fun. If you feed your crabs homegrown veggies, you'll know your pets are getting healthy, better tasting treats.

When growing vegetables for your crabs at home, do not use pesticides and insecticides on your plants. Crabs are particularly susceptible to these poisons, so keep these chemicals off your veggies. Instead, use biological controls to keep pests at bay, such as ladybugs and praying mantises, available at your local nursery.

Herbs

Herbs also make good treats for your crabs. When the leaves are chopped up small, they can be served to your crabs in a shallow food bowl. Herbs provide vitamins and minerals, and are full of flavor.

Some favorites crab herbs include parsley, cilantro, rosemary, and basil. Buy only fresh, organically grown herbs at a health food store, or grow your own and do not use any pesticides or insecticides. If you live in an apartment, you can grow herbs on a windowsill or fire escape.

Fruit

Hermit crabs love fruit, chopped in small pieces. They obtain fiber from fresh fruit, as well as vitamins and minerals.

Hermit crabs love fresh fruit, cut into small pieces.

Great Foods for Your Hermit Crabs

Greens

Green plants are good for hermit crabs because they provide plenty of vitamins and minerals. Since plant material is an important part of the hermit crab's diet in the wild, it is essential to regularly offer your crabs as many of the following greens as you can.

- Alfalfa sprouts
- Amaranth
- Arugula
- Basil
- Bok choy
- Broccoli
- Carrots (roots and tops)
- Celery
- Chard
- Cilantro
- Collard greens
- Cucumber
- Dandelion leaves
- Grape leaves
- Kale
- Kelp
- Parsley
- Romaine lettuce
- Rosemary
- Spinach
- Watercress
- Zucchini

Fruit

In their natural habitat, hermit crabs climb trees and eat the fruit that hangs, or find it below the tree after it has fallen.

Fruit is an important part of the hermit crab's diet, although it should be fed in moderation. Offer your hermit crabs some or all of the following fresh fruits no more than twice a week.

Buy your crabs' fruit at a health food store so you know you are getting organically grown produce. Another option is to feed your crab fruit from a backyard tree, whether yours or a neighbor's. Remember that fruit should not be treated with pesticides or insecticides for your crabs' safety.

Some favorite fruits for hermit crabs include bananas, apples, avocados, blackberries, blueberries, cantaloupe, cherries, cranberries, grapes, mangos, oranges, and peaches.

- Apple
- Avocado
- Banana
- Blackberries
- Blueberries
- Cantaloupe
- Carambola
- Cherries
- Coconut
- Cranberries
- Grapes
- Honeydew
- Mango
- Orange
- Papaya
- Peach
- Pear
- Pomegranate
- Raisins
- Watermelon

Protein

In nature, hermit crabs seek out sources of protein such as animal carcasses and feces. In captivity, hermit crabs need protein to stay healthy. Regularly offer your hermit crabs the following protein-rich items.

- Cat or dog food (soaked if dry, or canned)
- Chicken (cooked)
- Commercial hermit crab food (daily)
- Crickets
- Fish
- Beef
- Bloodworms
- Clams
- Freeze-dried plankton
- Freeze-dried shrimp
- Freeze-dried water fleas
- Eggs (cooked)
- Peanut butter
- Tropical fish food
- Turtle food

Fish and Turtle Food

Food made for aquarium fish can also be a good treat for hermit crabs, who will enjoy the added variety these items bring to their diet. Fish food is also fortified with vitamins and minerals, and so is a healthy treat.

Fish foods that are most enjoyed by hermit crabs include dried seaweed, any kind of fish flakes, and freeze-dried plankton, bloodworms, shrimp, and water fleas.

Commercial turtle food is another good treat for hermit crabs. If your crabs are small, be sure to crush up the pelleted food into a powder so the crabs can eat it.

People Food

Because hermit crabs are scavengers, they can eat just about anything we eat that is healthy. One big exception to this is dairy products. Hermit crabs do not have the capability to digest dairy foods such as milk and cheese, so don't give these items to your crabs. Sugar is also a no-no for hermit crabs, as are artificial sweeteners.

> **TIP**
>
> Feed people food in moderation and only as an occasional treat. Be sure to throw out uneaten food after a few hours so it doesn't spoil or attract flies and other pests.

Some examples of healthy human foods you can give to your crabs include almonds, walnuts, popcorn, breakfast cereals (containing barley, oats, wheat quinoa, or kashi, but no sugar), brown rice, cooked chicken, clams, cooked eggs, garbanzo beans (chickpeas), grape leaves, peanut butter, black olives, sunflower seeds, cooked corn, and sweet potatoes.

Leaves and Bark

Hermit crabs seem to be very fond of dried tree leaves, particularly oak tree leaves. They also like the leaves of raspberry bushes and tree bark. These items are rich in tannin, an ingredient that hermit crabs crave.

Before offering leaves and bark to your hermit crabs, be sure to wash the items thoroughly and allow them to dry.

Insects

In the wild, hermit crabs sometimes dine on live insects. To help simulate their natural diet, some hermit crab owners feed live insects to their crabs.

The best insects to offer hermit crabs are crickets. If your crabs are small, baby pinhead crickets are the best choice. If you have larger crabs, adult crickets are fine.

If you choose to offer your crabs wild-caught crickets, make sure the crickets have not been sprayed with an insecticide before you caught them. Insecticides are deadly to hermit crabs. The best way to do this is to collect the crickets from your own garden, or from a wild area that you know is not sprayed.

Clean bark and dried tree leaves make yummy snacks for your hermit crabs.

Only offer one or two crickets at a time to your hermit crabs, and remove the insects in a few hours if the crabs don't eat them. Crickets will defecate in the enclosure and foul the substrate if they spend any length of time there. They may also drown in your crabs' water dish.

If your crabs are having trouble catching the crickets or eating them when they are alive, you'll need to offer them dead crickets instead. These are often available at pet and aquarium supply stores.

Calcium

Hermit crabs need a source of calcium in their diets in order to stay healthy. In addition to feeding them green vegetables, which are high in calcium, you should also provide them with a cuttlebone. Cuttlebones are available in pet supply stores.

You can leave the cuttlebone in your crabs' enclosure until it's gone. This allows your pets to munch on it whenever they need more calcium in their diets.

As we've already mentioned, dairy products, while a good source of calcium for us, are not good for hermit crabs.

Recipes for Hermit Crabs

Some hermit crab owners like to make special recipes for their pets. Since hermit crabs have a widely varied diet, the possibilities for hermit crab recipes are almost endless. Just about anything goes, except sugar, sugar substitutes, and dairy products. Here are a few examples of hermit crab recipes that your pets will find healthy and tasty.

Fruit and Nut Salad

1 slice apple, finely chopped
½ banana, mashed
1 slice pear, finely chopped
1 pinch crushed almonds

Mix all the ingredients together in a bowl and offer to your crabs.

Shrimp and Egg Feast

1 egg
1 shrimp
1 pinch sea salt
1 teaspoon parsley, finely chopped

Boil the egg and shrimp separately. Peel the egg and mash it up. Remove the shell from the shrimp and chop the shrimp up in very fine pieces. Mix all the ingredients together and offer to your crabs.

Tuna and Veggie Casserole

2 tablespoons canned tuna
⅓ carrot, grated
⅛ teaspoon alfalfa powder
½ baked potato, mashed
2 spinach leaves

Boil the spinach leaves and chop into fine pieces, then mix with the mashed potato. Mash the tuna and add to the spinach leaves and potato. Add the grated carrot and alfalfa powder and mix well before serving.

Serving the Food

Your hermit crabs should always have some commercial crab food in their enclosure so they can eat whenever they want. If the food is moist, be sure to replace it daily because wet food will spoil over time.

Fresh food treats should be offered daily. Because hermit crabs are nocturnal, it's best to offer your pets' their meal of fresh foods when the sun goes down. Place a small amount of fresh food in a dish that is designed for hermit crabs (it will have a ramp or gradation to allow the crabs access) and place it in an area near where your crabs are resting. If the crabitat has more than two or three crabs, consider offering the food in more than one dish so all the crabs have room to eat.

Be sure to remove any uneaten fresh food within an hour of serving it to prevent it from spoiling and fouling your crabs' habitat. Wash the dishes with antibacterial soap and rinse thoroughly before using them again.

How Often?

Your hermit crabs may not eat a lot from day to day, but you should still offer them food every day. You'll get a feeling for how often your crabs want to eat as you spend more time with them. Feeding them in the evening, when they are most active, will increase the likelihood that they will eat—and that you'll be able to watch them do it.

Your hermit crabs should always have some commercial crab food available.

Give your pets a small serving of commercial crab food in a shallow dish, along with some of the other foods mentioned in this chapter. Throw out the uneaten commercial food after a few hours.

Water

Hermit crabs are born in the ocean and are very dependent on water for their well-being. They will sit and soak in it, as well as drink it. Therefore, it's crucial they have a supply of water, both fresh and salt, in their crabitat at all times.

> **CAUTION**
>
> *Never* use table salt to make your crabs' salt water. Table salt contains iodine, which is harmful to crabs.

Provide your crabs with at least two shallow water dishes: one containing fresh water and the other containing seawater. The fresh water should be treated with a chlorine remover. You can buy chlorine remover designed for pets' drinking water at your pet supply store, in the aquarium fish department.

You don't need to make a trip to the ocean for your crab's supply of seawater. Products are available at pet supply stores that enable you to make salt water from fresh water. These products are designed for marine aquariums but also work well for creating salt water for hermit crabs.

Your crabs need both fresh water and salt water in their crabitat at all times, so they can drink and soak.

Follow the directions on the label and give your crabs a fresh supply of this salted water daily to keep them healthy. You can even make up a large batch and freeze it for future use. (If the crabs in your enclosure are of the *Coenobita compressus*—purple claw or Caribbean hermit crab—species, use a little bit less salt when you prepare the mixture.)

Chapter 7

Your Hermit Crab's Shell

If there's one thing hermit crabs are famous for, it's their shells. The shells of hermit crabs—the borrowed homes of sea creatures—have been a subject of fascination for centuries. The anatomy of the hermit crab requires these crustaceans to carry around a shell that is not their own. The hermit crab has a delicate abdomen that lacks the hard tissue that covers the rest of the crab's body. Why Mother Nature didn't give the hermit crab his own protective covering is a mystery, but she did give the crab an intense instinct to find and inhabit an empty one.

Hermit crabs use their shells not only to protect their abdomen from danger, but also to keep their bodies moist. They begin their existence in the ocean, and although they venture out onto land as soon as they mature, their need for water remains. Hermit crabs keep water inside their shells to prevent their formerly sea-faring bodies from drying out.

Selecting Shells

Hermit crabs are born in the ocean as free-swimming organisms, but when they mature, they begin their search for a shell to occupy. This quest begins underwater before the crab makes his way to land. Young hermit crabs usually inhabit the vacated shells of sea snails, which can be found in shallow ocean waters.

Once the crab has found a shell and crawls onto land, he continues to grow. Through a series of molts, the crab continues to get bigger and venture farther from the ocean. With each molt, the crab requires a bigger shell to house his growing body. When a shell is too small for a growing crab, he abandons that shell and seeks a larger one. Hermit crabs continually change shells throughout their lives.

The Crabs Choose

Although many new hermit crab owners have ideas about which shells they want their pets to occupy, the crabs are the only ones who can decide which shells they want.

When a hermit crab selects a shell, he takes several factors into consideration. First, the crab looks for a shell that is large enough to accommodate his body, yet not so large that he won't be able to store water in the shell. If a shell is the right fit, the crab will be able to retreat all the way into it, covering the opening with his large claw and second walking foot. If the crab is unable to retreat all the way into the shell, it's too small for that particular crab.

The opening of the shell is also a factor. The crab wants a shell that will have an opening large enough for him to enter through it yet small enough to be closed off using his large claw and second walking leg.

Ease of movement is another consideration for crabs, who want a shell that is easy to tote around. A shell that is too heavy or has a shape that requires the crab to drag it around with great effort will ultimately be rejected.

Typically, hermit crabs prefer the shells of marine snails, and will even inhabit the shells of land snails.

Only the crab knows what makes a shell the perfect home, so be sure to give your pet plenty of choices.

The crab on the right is moving out of his small shell and into a larger one. Hermit crabs need new shells periodically throughout their lives.

Shell Choice by Species

The two most common species of hermit crab kept as pets in North America, *Coenobita clypeatus* and *Coenobita compressus,* have slightly different tastes when it comes to shell choices.

C. clypeatus, the larger of the two species, prefers bigger shells with a round opening approximately 1½ to 2 inches in diameter. This size is for fully grown *C. clypeatus.* Juveniles of this species will be smaller and will therefore need a smaller shell.

C. compressus is small even at maturity, and prefers a shell that has an opening diameter of around half an inch. These crabs also seem to prefer shell openings that are more oblong, rather than round, because their heads and bodies are flatter.

Some crab owners have found that both species are especially drawn to shells that have a mother-of-pearl surface inside them, particularly at the opening. This smooth finish may provide more insulation for the crab, as well as a more comfortable fit.

Remodeling

Once a hermit crab chooses a shell he likes, he will begin a remodeling project on the interior to make it more comfortable and accommodating. He starts by removing something called the columella, a small columnlike structure inside

---

Entering the Shell

If you are lucky enough to see one of your hermit crabs move into a new shell, you'll notice that he carefully explores the shell first with his claws. He then holds onto the new shell while remaining in the old one. When the crab makes the switch, he does so quickly, backing into the new home, abdomen first. The reason for this is to minimize the amount of time the crab's tender abdomen is exposed to the open air—and to predators.

---

the shell. The crab may also enlarge the entrance of the shell to enable him to keep it longer as he grows.

Once a shell has been modified by its original hermit crab owner, it becomes a valuable commodity to other crabs. If the shell is ever abandoned, another crab will quickly claim ownership of it because of its exceptional added features.

Shells for Your Crabs

One of the most entertaining aspects of hermit crab ownership is watching your crab haul around his shell. Many owners enjoy providing their crabs with colorful, painted shells, or natural shells of great beauty. However, it's important to realize that your hermit crab will choose the shell he feels most comfortable in, and not necessarily the one you pick for him.

Shell Variety

Because hermit crabs change shells many times throughout their lives, it's important to provide them with a number of shells to choose from. Leave several shells of different sizes and shapes in your crabitat so your crabs can pick the ones they like most. Keep in mind that land hermit crabs prefer round snail shells—the kind that have concentric spiral coils. You can offer your pets other kinds of more decorative shells, however, and see if the crabs like them.

Watch your crabs as they try on different shells, exploring which ones might make the best home. You may find that after checking out a number of different shells, your crab goes back to his old one.

Painting the Shells

Some hermit crab owners like to give their crabs painted shells, but this practice is controversial in the hermit crab world. Many hermit crab owners believe that painted shells can be harmful to the crabs. Crabs have become trapped inside painted shells, and the paint can sometimes chip off and foul the crabs' water. Also, when given a choice, many crabs seem to prefer natural, unpainted shells.

If you feel strongly about painting the shells you offer your crabs and plan to paint them yourself, do so before offering them to your crabs. *Never paint a shell while a crab is in it*. And disinfect the shell first before you paint.

It's best to buy special hermit crab shell-painting kits, which include non-toxic paints. If you paint the shells yourself, be sure to only paint the outside of the shell. The interior should remain natural. Paint on the inside of the shell may harm your hermit crab. (This also applies to shells you buy that are already painted.) Be sure there is no paint near the opening of the shell, either, which might cause your crab to get stuck.

Before offering a painted shell to your crab, make sure the paint is completely dry. Wait at least two days after painting to be sure. Use only paints that are waterproof and non-toxic.

Buying Shells

It's easy to find shells for hermit crabs these days. Pet supply stores sell shells just for hermit crabs. You can also buy shells from shell stores, both in person and on the Internet.

Please resist the urge to go down to the beach to collect shells from the shoreline or tide pools. Wild hermit crabs need those shells for their own use. In fact, shell collection is one of the reasons some hermit crabs are having difficulty surviving in the wild.

When choosing shells to buy for your crabs, consider the width of your crabs' large claw. Look for shells that have openings that can easily be covered by the crabs' large claw, yet are big enough to allow the crab easy entry.

Preparing the Shells

Before offering shells to your crabs, be sure to clean them first to make sure no bacteria is lurking inside. You can disinfect them by boiling them in water for fifteen minutes. Leave them to dry and cool down before placing them in the crabitat.

If you plan to paint the shells before offering them to your crabs (see "Painting the Shells," in this chapter for more information), disinfect them before you paint.

Look for shells that have openings that can easily be covered by a crab's large claw, yet are big enough to allow a crab easy entry.

Avoiding Shell Fights

Another reason it's vital to give your crabs several shells they can explore as possible homes is to prevent shell fights. Hermit crabs spend their lives looking for better shells, and if a crab decides that his tankmate has a better shell than he does, he will fight in an attempt to make that shell his own. The need for a better shell is determined by how well the current shell fits and whether it is damaged. Hermit crabs don't like damaged shells because they provide less protection from predators and dehydration.

Shell fights can be deadly to the weaker crab, and at the very least, can cause both crabs to lose limbs. It's vital to prevent these duels among your crabs.

> **TIP**
>
> Don't be surprised if one crab's entry into a new shell causes a domino effect of shell swapping among all your crabs.

To avoid these battles, place at least two extra shells per crab in your crabitat. If you see a crab fighting another one, even if there are extra shells, separate the aggressor crab and offer him several more empty shells to choose from.

Keeping Shells Wet

Hermit crabs need to store water in their shells to keep their gills wet and make breathing easier. This stored water also helps keep them from dehydrating. When you think about the fact that hermit crabs begin their lives underwater, it's not hard to understand why it's vital for them to keep the insides of their shells wet.

Crabs work hard to keep water inside their shells. You may see your crab immerse himself in his water dish and shovel water into his shell and his mouth using his claws.

Once the water enters the shell, a rhythmic motion of the crab's abdomen pushes the water back so it fills the open area in the crab's shell, between the abdomen and the inside of the shell. Just enough water enters the shell to enable the crab's abdomen to keep the water inside and prevent it from evaporating rapidly.

Crabs are good at moving around their environment without spilling any of the water they keep in their shells. Some water may leak out if the crab retreats deep into the shell, however, forcing the crab to replenish the water supply as quickly as possible.

Offer plenty of shells to your crabs to avoid shell fights.

Chapter 8

Keeping Your Hermit Crabs Healthy

If you take good care of your crabs and provide them with everything they need to survive, you may be lucky enough to have them live ten years or longer. Occasionally, hermit crabs do get sick. Although they are hardy creatures, they can only take so much in the way of inadequate care before illness catches up to them.

Prevention Is Everything

Everyone knows that if a dog or cat gets sick, you can take the pet to a veterinarian. Veterinarians rarely see sick hermit crabs, though. The low cost of hermit crabs, combined with the relatively high cost of veterinary care, mean most hermit crab owners never consider taking their crabs to a vet. Consequently, the veterinary community knows very little about how to treat hermit crabs.

Some veterinarians who specialize in caring for exotic pets will do their best to treat hermit crabs who are sick, but since not much is known about hermit crab diseases and how to treat them, your vet will be very limited in what he or she is able to do to help your pet.

The saying "An ounce of prevention is worth a pound of cure" was never more true than when it comes to hermit crabs. Because veterinary knowledge about how to treat sick crabs is hard to come by, it's vital to keep your crab from becoming ill in the first place.

Signs of a Sick Crab

Hermit crabs can't talk, so we have to depend on their behavior to signal us when something is amiss with their physical well-being. Here are some signs that your crab is not feeling well:

- **Refusal to eat.** Crabs who are sick will ignore their food for days at a time and will become weaker as a result. (Since most crabs don't eat every day, it's important to get to know your crabs' behavior so you can detect when one is not eating normally.)
- **Sluggishness.** Sick crabs tend to hide in their shells and don't move around much. If you see that one of your crabs is listless and withdrawn, something is amiss. (She may also be preparing to molt; see page 91.)
- **Lack of antennae activity.** Healthy crabs constantly wiggle their antennae. If a crab is listless and her antennae aren't moving, she's not feeling well. (She may also be preparing to molt; see page 91.)
- **Lost limbs.** Crabs who are stressed or wounded will sometimes lose one or more legs or a claw.

Crab Troubles

Hermit crabs are susceptible to several maladies, some of which may be helped by changing the crab's environment. Keep a close eye on your crabs' behavior to help determine if one is suffering from one of the following health problems.

Dehydration

Even though land hermit crabs live on dry ground, they are highly dependent on moisture for their survival. Without sufficient humidity in their environment and moisture in their shells, hermit crabs cannot breathe properly. They will also dehydrate as the moisture evaporates from their bodies. *Lack of humidity is fatal to hermit crabs.*

If your crab is showing signs of illness, suspect lack of humidity in her environment as a culprit. If you don't already have one, buy a humidity gauge for your crab's tank (sold at pet supply stores) and check the current humidity levels. If the gauge indicates the level of relative humidity is below 79 percent,

A swim in a shallow dish of water may help a crab who is feeling dehydrated.

rectify the situation immediately by spraying the inside of the tank with water. (Avoid dampening the substrate, since you don't want it to become soggy.) Add dishes of water to the crabitat to help provide humidity and limit the amount of airflow inside the tank to keep moisture from escaping.

It may also be a good idea to dip your ill hermit crab in a dish of shallow, lukewarm water to help rehydrate her.

If these efforts seem to revive your crab, be sure to continue with this regimen to make sure your crab stays healthy. Since dehydration is extremely harmful to crabs, be aware that your pet may not survive.

Chilling

Hermit crabs are native to tropical climates, so they need to be kept warm at all times. Unlike cats, dogs, and other mammals, hermit crabs and all crustaceans are cold-blooded, and can't generate their own body heat. They are completely dependent on a heat source within their environment for their bodily functions to work.

If your hermit crab is not eating and is inactive, she may be suffering from a too-cold environment. If you don't already have one, purchase a tank thermometer at your local pet supply store. The temperature inside the tank should be between 76 and 82 degrees Fahrenheit. If the temperature is lower than this, your crab is too cold. (If the temperature is above 82, your crab may be too hot.)

If you don't already have one, purchase a heating element for your crabitat right away. Undertank heating pads are the best choice for a hermit crab enclosure.

Be sure to insulate the tank too, to help keep the temperature in the desired 76- to 82-degree range. You can do this with foam board taped to three sides of the exterior glass.

If your crab begins to eat and move around once you warm her up, cold may have been her problem. Be sure to keep her tank at the right temperature in the future to keep her healthy.

To Bathe or Not to Bathe

Some people believe hermit crabs should receive "baths" once a week. These baths consist of dipping the crab and her shell into a shallow dish of water and allowing the shell to fill up. The shell is then tipped so the water comes out and the crab is allowed to dry on her own.

Hermit crab owners who advocate weekly baths believe this practice helps their pets stay well-hydrated. Baths seem to stimulate the crabs too, encouraging them to heightened activity for a period of time after the bath.

Those who do not believe hermit crabs need baths believe the activity stresses the crab. They also say that if your crabitat humidity levels are as they should be, you have no reason to dip your crab in water once a week.

The question of whether or not to bathe your crab is an individual one, based on your preferences as a crab owner.

If you choose to give your crabs a dip once a week, be sure to use dechlorinated lukewarm water. Never hold a crab under the water, since she will drown if submerged. And remember that weekly baths cannot make up for low humidity levels in the crabitat.

Malnutrition

Just like us, hermit crabs require a varied diet to get the nutrition they need. In the wild, they eat just about anything. If your hermit crab seems listless and you have checked that the heat and humidity in her enclosure are what they should be, take a look at what you are feeding her.

In addition to a commercial hermit crab diet (available in pet supply stores), your pet should be offered vegetables, fruit, nuts, and other healthy, natural foods. You should not be giving your crab anything that contains dairy products or sugar. (See chapter 6 for more information on what to feed your hermit crabs.)

There's no substitute for a healthy, varied diet for your crabs.

Calcium is another important element that all hermit crabs need in their diet. Provide your crab with a cuttlebone in her enclosure at all times so she will have access to a good source of calcium when she needs it.

If you crab's diet is not what it should be, start feeding her appropriate foods and see if she perks up after a week or so. Be diligent about always offering her fresh foods, and be sure to clean up uneaten meals within an hour of offering them.

Lost Limbs

Hermit crabs sometimes lose one or more of their limbs. You may find your crab with one leg missing, or several legs gone. You may even see a pincher missing.

Sometimes, lost limbs indicate a problem in the crab's environment, such as not enough heat and/or humidity, or poor nutrition. Psychological stress can also cause a crab to lose limbs. Crabs sometimes lose legs when they are undergoing a transition from one home to another. It's not uncommon to buy a new

Limb Regrowth

If you find a stray limb in the crabitat or notice that one of your crabs has lost a leg, don't panic. Unlike us mammals, hermit crabs can regrow lost limbs.

When a leg breaks off, a gel-like scab forms over the open wound to prevent blood loss. Gradually, a new leg will start to grow. It might take a while for the leg to fully grow back.

Do worry if a crab loses several legs in a day. If this happens, she is most likely dying. You should isolate this ailing crab, offering her food and water, but know that recovery isn't likely. If the crab dies, check your other crabs closely, and check the tank for mites and other parasites.

crab and then, over the next month, find that one leg or more is missing. Illness or injury can also cause a crab to drop her limbs.

Occasionally, hermit crabs lose limbs when they molt. When the crab emerges from her molt, she may have a leg or two gone.

The good news is that hermit crabs have regenerating powers and can regrow their limbs. If they are kept in a good environment and fed a healthy diet, the missing limbs will start to grow back and the crabs will eventually be as good as new.

Mites

The warm, moist environment hermit crabs need to stay healthy also attracts parasites known as mites. You may see these tiny arachnids (relatives of the spider) crawling around on your hermit crab and inside her crabitat.

Mites are unsightly and unpleasant to have around, but that's not the worst of it. Mites can get under a crab's shell and feed off the crab and eat her food. A crab under stress from other factors who is also exposed to mites might lose legs, stop eating, or even die. Molting crabs are particularly vulnerable to mite attacks.

Unfortunately, getting rid of mites isn't easy because the commercial products designed to kill mites are also harmful to hermit crabs. You can try several methods to rid your crabitat of these pests. First, remove your crabs and put them in a safe place, such as a small carrier lined with paper towels.

If you find mites in the crabitat, you'll have to throw away all wood decorations and climbing sticks.

Dispose of the substrate by dumping it in the trash, outside your home. If you have expensive substrate that you don't want to throw out, you can sterilize it by baking it in your oven at 300 degrees Fahrenheit for thirty minutes. Make sure you spread the substrate thinly on a cookie sheet before you bake it. Let it cool thoroughly before you put in back in the tank.

The tank should also be cleaned out thoroughly. Wash it out with hot water mixed with white vinegar, and, using paper towels, clean the corners and any areas where mites might be hiding. Rinse very thoroughly until no vinegar smell remains. Do not use household cleaning products to clean the crabitat, because the residue they invariably leave behind can kill your crabs.

> **TIP**
>
> Use duct tape to tape down the cra-bitat cover. It peels back easily for daily access, keeps the lid secure, and the adhesive traps mites before they have a chance to crawl in.

Since mites are attracted to wood, dispose of any wood toys, decorations, or climbing areas that were inside your crabitat. (If the substrate was wood, be sure to replace it with sand or another non-wood substrate.)

Your crabs' hiding places, extra shells, and other tank accessories should be boiled for several minutes to rid them of mites. Since you can't boil plastic items, these should be thrown away and replaced.

You'll need to get the mites off your crabs, too. You can best do this by soaking your crabs in lukewarm warm for a few minutes. (Be sure not to submerge your pets; they will drown.) The mites will abandon ship and float to the top of the water, at which time you can dump the water in the sink. Do this a couple of times for each crab until no more mites show up in the water.

To prevent mites from reinfesting your crabitat, keep your tank as clean as possible, remove uneaten food in a timely manner, and clean up crab waste at least once a day, if not more. Avoid putting wood objects in your crabitat, as these will attract mites.

Shell Disease

A serious malady affecting hermit crabs is something called shell disease. Also known as black spot, rust spot, or shell rot, shell disease is a generic term for any kind of bacterial or fungal infection that penetrates the crab's chitin (the outer shell layer). Hermit crabs are not the only creatures affected by this malady. Lobsters and crayfish also have problems with shell disease.

Hermit crabs suffering from shell disease have discolored areas on their bodies, and may also have pockmarks. This malady most often affects crabs who are injured or stressed.

Proper care, including regular misting, will help your crabs avoid shell disease.

What Healthy Crabs Need

Hermit crabs are such popular pets in large part because they are so easy to keep. Under the right conditions, hermit crabs rarely get sick and can live up to ten years or longer.

The key to such a long life span for hermit crabs is keeping them in the right environment. They need the right substrate, heat, humidity, and diet to live a healthy life.

If you find your hermit crabs are having health issues, take a look at the way you are maintaining their crabitat. Examine the following issues:

- **Humidity.** Hermit crabs need to live in a relative humidity range of 79 to 90 percent. Without this moisture, they can dehydrate and die. Spray the crabitat with water every evening to keep it moist, and add dishes of water that will help provide humidity through evaporation. Use a humidity gauge to make sure humidity stays at the correct level.
- **Heat.** Hermit crabs are native to warm climates and need heat in their environment to function properly. Provide your crabs with a source of heat in the form of an undertank heating pad or other type of heating element. Use insulation around the outside of the

Thought to be caused by bacteria that infect the chitinous layers of the hermit crab's outer body, shell disease is usually fatal. No cure has been discovered for this disease, although some crab owners have experimented with dipping crabs in saline solution or medicated water (treated with antibiotics designed for use in aquarium fish), with mixed results.

If you suspect one of your hermit crabs has shell disease, separate her from the other crabs immediately, as this disease is thought to be contagious. Keep her in a warm, humid environment tank of her own, working to keep her stress levels to a minimum. Be prepared to lose the crab, since most crabs are unsuccessful at fighting off this disease, especially if the condition is advanced.

To help ensure your other crabs don't develop shell disease, provide them with the heat, humidity, and water they need. Prevent injuries by discouraging shell fights. You can do this by offering a lot of empty shells for your crabs to choose from.

tank to help keep the heat inside. Monitor the temperature with a tank thermometer. Your crabs' enclosure should be kept somewhere between 76 and 82 degrees Fahrenheit.

- **Diet.** Hermit crabs need a varied diet that includes protein and plant material. Offer your hermit crabs fresh fruit and vegetables, plus a staple of a quality commercial hermit crab food.
- **Water.** Because hermit crabs are born in the water, they need a constant source of both fresh water and salt water in their tanks. Provide both types of water in shallow dishes.
- **Stress.** Constant stress can be a killer for hermit crabs. Crabs become stressed when they are overcrowded, are bullied by larger crabs, are handled too much, or don't have enough shells to choose from. Keep your crab population to a minimum while also providing plenty of shells for crabs to pick from while they are growing. Try to keep crabs of the same size together in one tank.
- **Tank hygiene.** It's important to keep your crabs' tank clean and free of uneaten food and waste. Daily clean-ups will help keep the crabitat free of bacteria and disease.
- **Harmful substances.** Keep hermit crabs far away from household cleaners, aerosol sprays, and insecticides. These products can enter your crabs' enclosure and make them ill.

Out of the Shell

Hermit crabs sometimes come out of their shells and act panicky. It's no wonder the crab acts frantic when she's outside her shell, since hermit crabs need to be inside their shells to survive. A crab without a shell won't last too long.

It's important to help your crab get back into a shell and then figure out why your crab abandoned her shell in the first place. Encourage your crab to go back into a shell (either her old one or a new one) by placing her in a small container with several shells that have been washed in lukewarm water. Put the container in a dark place to help reduce the crab's stress level. Check on her every so often and give her a spray of dechlorinated water to keep her from becoming dehydrated.

You can also try gently tapping your crab on the head with your finger. This may encourage her to go back to her shell. Give her some time to choose and reinhabit one of these shells. Once she's inside, you can put her back in the main enclosure with your other crabs.

Regularly cleaning the crabitat will go a long way toward keeping your crabs healthy. Put them in a temporary carrier so you can clean everything, including the substrate.

Once you've handled the crisis, it's time to figure out what happened. Hermit crabs leave their shells for several reasons, including the following:

- **Stressful environment.** The crabitat may be too warm. Check the temperature and make sure it's not over 82 degrees Fahrenheit. If the enclosure is too hot, gradually cool it down by providing more ventilation, being careful not to go below 76 degrees.
- **Lost shell.** Take a look around to see if another one of your crabs has confiscated your "naked" crab's shell. Larger, more aggressive crabs will sometimes steal the shells of weaker individuals. To discourage this, keep a number of extra shells in the crabitat.
- **Problem with the shell.** There may be something wrong with the shell she was occupying, which prompted her to abandon it before finding a new one. Examine the shell for sand or any kind of material that may be irritating your crab's delicate abdomen. Look for mites, too, since a severe mite infestation inside the shell may have prompted your crab to move out.
- **Shell is too small.** If your hermit crab has outgrown her shell and doesn't have a suitable one to move into, she may end up shell-less. Provide her with a number of different shells to choose from if she doesn't want to go back to her original home.

Molting

In crabs, molting is the shedding of the exoskeleton to allow a new, larger one to grow. When a crab molts, she is exchanging her old skeleton for a newer one that is bigger.

Molting is an important time for hermit crabs. They are very vulnerable during this period. They become sluggish and sometimes completely inactive for several days, making them vulnerable to predators. Because their protective exoskeletons are discarded and it takes awhile for the new exoskeleton to harden, they are also susceptible to pests, illnesses, and other crabs.

Hermit crabs molt in their shells, and do it about once every one to two years, on average, depending on their size and the conditions in their environment. Crabs kept in a healthy crabitat will molt more often than those kept under less-than-optimum conditions.

Molting crabs need extra care, so it's important that you learn to recognize the signs of an impending molt and know what to do to help your crab. Be sure to provide the optimum environment for your crab so she will be successful in achieving her next level of growth.

Preparing to Molt

When hermit crabs are preparing to molt, their behavior and physical appearance changes somewhat a few weeks beforehand. Learn to recognize the signs of an impending molt.

- **Increased water intake.** Hermit crabs who are getting ready to molt drink a lot of water. You'll see your hermit crab spending a lot of time in her water dish.
- **Digging.** Hermit crabs like to bury themselves before they molt. If you see your crab doing a lot of digging, she is most like preparing to shed her skin.
- **Increased appetite.** Some hermit crabs become very hungry just before they molt and will eat a lot more than usual.

A crab preparing to molt may be less active and even withdrawn.

Molting, Not Dead!

The signs of an impending molt look a like the signs of impending death in hermit crabs, which has caused more than one hermit crab owner to assume their pet had passed on, when the crab was, in fact, just molting. One hermit crab owner went so far as to bury her "dead" hermit crab in the backyard, only to discover the crab walking around the yard a few days later with a fresh new skin.

To determine if your crab is molting or preparing to move to the great beyond, look for increased water intake before the crab's appearance of "near death." Look for a lot of digging activity, as well. Crabs who are about to molt will dig deep into the substrate.

If your crab isn't moving and you aren't sure if she's dead or just molting, use your nose as a guide. A dead crab will have a fishy odor, while a molting crab will have a slight smell of iodine or no odor at all.

If you are in doubt about whether your crab is dead or molting, wait a few days to see if she revives.

- **Lethargy.** As molting time approaches, hermit crabs appear sluggish and lethargic.
- **Gel limbs.** Crabs who are missing limbs may start to grow gel-like nubs where their missing limbs once were. These crabs are getting ready to molt and grow a new limb.
- **Development of a pericardial sac.** Just before they molt, hermit crabs develop a pericardial sac, which looks like a small, dark-colored balloon on the abdomen, near the legs. This sac contains water that will help the crab get through the molting process. Although all crabs develop this sac before molting, you may have trouble seeing the sac. Don't assume your crab isn't about to molt just because the sac isn't visible.

In Mid-Molt

Sometimes crab owners don't know their crabs are going to molt, but will find them one day in full molt. These signs indicate your crab is molting or has just molted.

- **No movement.** The crab is not moving at all, not even her antennae. She doesn't respond when you touch her.
- **Dull eyes and/or exoskeleton.** Molting crabs have a fuzzy look, as if they are covered with a fungus. This is actually the old exoskeleton, which is starting to shed.
- **Discarded exoskeleton.** The crab's entire exoskeleton may be discarded from her body.
- **Tangled antennae.** The crab's antennae may be twisted up and bent.

Isolating the Crab

If you have determined that your crab is getting ready to molt, or if you find your crab already molting, it's important to separate her from the other crabs in her enclosure. The reason for this is that crabs are at their most vulnerable and may be attacked or even eaten by other crabs during this stage of growth.

Some crab owners place their molting crabs in a separate tank set aside just for molting. This enclosure serves only as a temporary tank. To set up a molting tank, you'll need the following:

- **A small aquarium.** A 2- or 5-gallon aquarium will be sufficient as a molting tank, since it is temporary and is for crabs who are essentially immobile. Although your crab shouldn't be in the mood to climb out while she's molting, it's a good idea to keep the enclosure securely covered just in case. A cover will also help keep humidity inside.
- **A heating element.** A small undertank heating element should keep the tank warm. The temperature should be maintained at the same range as the permanent crabitat (76 to 82 degrees Fahrenheit).
- **Deep substrate.** Molting crabs like to bury themselves in the substrate. Use sand or another material that is easy to dig through (gravel is too big). The substrate should be at least 6 inches deep in the molting tank.
- **Water dishes.** Include two shallow water dishes in your crab's molting tank—one for fresh water and one for salt water. Keep these filled while your crab is molting.

- **Food dish.** A shallow food dish should be a part of your crab's molting tank, since she will be hungry both before and after her molt.
- **A hiding place.** Be sure to give your crab a hiding place where she can stash herself away when she's not buried under the substrate.

Place your crab in the molting tank as soon as you see signs that she is ready to molt. Keep the inside of the tank humid, using the same methods you use for your regular crabitat (see chapter 5, "A Home for Your Hermit Crabs," for details). Use a thermometer and humidity gauge to keep track of the heat and moisture levels inside the tank. Even though your crab is molting, she still needs the same air temperature and humidity she would have in her regular enclosure.

If your crab is still active, offer her food while she's in the molting tank. Once she stops eating, don't give her anything more to eat, since it will just spoil in the warm, damp environment.

If you discover your crab is already molting, you may opt to keep her in the permanent enclosure with your other crabs as long as you put up a barrier to keep the other crabs away from her. You can use a piece of Plexiglas, heavy cardboard, or another sturdy barrier. Make sure the barrier reaches all the way from

Molting crabs like to bury themselves deep in the substrate.

the base of the aquarium to the top. You don't want other crabs to be able to dig their way underneath it or climb over the top.

In the separate area you have set up for your molting crab, include two water dishes (one with fresh water and one with salt water), a food dish, and a hiding place. If your crab has already dug into the substrate, leave her there. If she's looking for a place to dig, give her deep substrate so she can cover herself.

If you are using a barrier that may keep the heat and moisture from the rest of the tank out, be sure to monitor the heat and humidity in this separate area of the tank.

After the Molt

You'll know your hermit crab has completed her molting when she has completely shed her old exoskeleton. You may be tempted to return her to the community of other crabs, but she should stay isolated for about ten days. That's because it will take her new exoskeleton some time to harden and become strong enough to withstand any altercations with other crabs.

Your newly molted crab needs water and nutrition, so be sure to keep both fresh and salt water in her molting tank, as well as offering her food each day.

After your crab's new exoskeleton has hardened and she seems to be back to normal, you can return her to her permanent enclosure.

> **TIP**
>
> Do not discard your crab's exoskeleton after she completes a molt. This old exoskeleton contains a lot of nutrients, including calcium. Leave it inside your crabitat so she can eat it when she's ready.

Part III

Enjoying Your Hermit Crabs

Chapter 9

Hermit Crab Behavior

Hermit crab owners around the world love to watch their crabs. Despite the fact that they are rather primitive creatures, hermit crabs engage in a number of fascinating behaviors. If you spend time watching your hermit crabs, you'll come to know each individual crab well and will recognize typical hermit crab behaviors.

Socializing

You know by now that hermit crabs do best when they share their homes with other hermit crabs. That's because these interesting creatures are highly social with one another.

In the wild, hermit crabs live in large groups and interact with one another regularly. In captivity, hermit crabs do the same. They rub antennae with other crabs, crawl all over each other, and basically act like they all are part of one big group—which they are.

If you take the time to observe your crabs in the evening hours, you'll see them interacting as only hermit crabs can. You'll watch them do things such as gang up to knock over items in their crabitat by piling on top of each other, gather together in the food dish to share a treat you may have given them, and simply greet one another with antennae waving.

Eating

Watching your hermit crabs eat is one of the most enjoyable aspects of owning these special crustaceans. Hermit crabs have a fascinating way of partaking in meals.

They are good at knowing what kind of food you have placed in their crabitats, since they have the ability to see and smell food from as far as 6 feet away. If you put something that is particularly fragrant in their food dish after sunset, you'll no doubt see your crabs come forward to investigate. Hermit crabs also respond to the sight of other hermit crabs eating, so you are likely to see more than one crab feasting at a time.

> **They Love the Night Life**
>
> Hermit crabs are nocturnal and so are most active after the sun goes down. In the wild, being nocturnal is a matter of survival, since the tropical sun in their native habitat can easily dehydrate them. Coming out at night reduces the likelihood that the crabs will dry out.

When hermit crabs eat, they pick the food up with their claws and put it to their mouths. You can enjoy watching your hermit crab "shovel" his food into his mouth. Favorite foods go down the hatch faster than more boring (by crab standards) items.

Self-Grooming

Although they might not be as fastidious as cats, hermit crabs do like to keep themselves clean. Self-grooming is one of the many interesting behaviors you will see in your hermit crabs.

Crabs with clean body parts are able to see and function better in their environment. Keeping the inside of the shell clean is also useful for hermit crabs, since it prevents sand and other irritants from building up inside where these particles can irritate the crab's tender abdomen.

For these reasons, crabs focus on keeping their claws, legs, eye stalks, antennae, and interior shells clean. They groom their claws by picking dirt and sand out of the crevices with their opposing claw. Crabs clean their legs by rubbing them on each other. Their eye stalks and antennae are rubbed clean using their legs.

Cleaning the interior of the shell requires a different approach. The crab uses his back legs to scrape the inside of the shell, pushing out any debris that may be lodged inside. The opening of the shell is kept clean using the small claw. You may not know your crab is cleaning the inside of his shell because you won't be able to see what is going on, but if he appears to be doing *something* inside there, he is most likely cleaning house.

Climbing

Hermit crabs love to climb. In the wild, many hermit crabs use this skill to climb trees looking for food. In captivity, hermit crabs show their love of climbing by scaling anything they can get their claws on.

If you have provided some climbing areas for your hermit crabs in their crabitat, you'll see them showing off their skills regularly. Climbing mats, textured ornaments, and even screen tops are all suitable climbing surfaces for hermit crabs. In fact, hermit crabs are such good climbers that it's important to keep the top of your tank securely fastened. Otherwise, your crabs may climb right out of their crabitat!

Crabs are able to climb by hooking the tips of their legs onto small protrusions on a vertical surface. They hoist themselves up, shell and all, and climb using these natural rungs in whatever they are climbing.

In the wild, many hermit crabs climb trees to look for food. Make sure your pets have plenty of climbing surfaces.

Hermit crabs have also been known to climb to the screen tops of aquariums, positioning themselves upside down and holding on.

Climbing is a strenuous activity for a hermit crab. You may see your pet take a snooze on a vertical surface, once he has climbed as high as he wants to.

Digging

Digging is another important crab behavior. Hermit crabs dig to get past an object that's in their way (often instead of simply going around it), to bury their bodies to cool themselves off when they are feeling warm, and to hide.

When hermit crabs dig, they use their pinchers to move substrate out of the way. They prefer to dig in moist areas, which is why owners often find their crabs' water dishes knocked over in the mornings when they come to check on their pets. If the substrate around the water dish is damp, the crabs will dig into it. Likewise, if the water dish crosses their path and the substrate is damp around it, they will dig underneath, upsetting the dish.

Some hermit crab owners report that their crabs deliberately dampen areas of substrate by filling their shells with water from the dish and then crawling to another area, where they let the water dribble out. The crabs then dig in the damp substrate.

Hermit crabs really enjoy digging, which is one reason why sand is an excellent substrate for the crabitat.

Because hermit crabs enjoy digging so much, it's important to provide them with substrate they can easily move with their tiny pinchers. For optimal digging conditions, I recommend at least 4 to 5 inches of substrate for smaller crabs. If you're housing larger crabs, the substrate should be 7 to 10 inches deep.

Aggression

While most hermit crab behaviors are endearing, one common behavior is not. Crab-on-crab aggression is not only upsetting to owners, but it can be deadly to crabs.

When crabs become aggressive, they typically attack other crabs by pulling at them with their pinchers. Crabs sometimes flip other crabs onto their backs in an attempt to ward off the victim crab's defensive pincher.

A great many crab fights are actually shell fights, where one crab tries to steal the shell of another crab (see chapter 7, "Your Hermit Crab's Shell," for advice on how to avoid shell fights). The aggressor crab tries to pull the victim crab out of his shell by grabbing with a pincher and pulling. In defense, the victim crab will withdraw into his shell as far as he will go. If the aggressor persists, the victim crab may drop a limb in an attempt to dislodge the aggressor's grip.

Crabs sometimes fight for reasons unknown to their human caretakers, attacking each other's eyes, antennae, and limbs. The result can be severe injury that can result in infection and ultimate death for the losing crab.

If you see one of your crabs engaging in aggressive behavior toward another crab, separate the two immediately. Put the aggressive crab in a dark, quiet place, such as a small molting tank or a travel carrier. Let the crab calm down before you return him to the enclosure.

If the aggression persists and seems to be a shell fight (the aggressor is trying to pull the other crab out of his shell), separate the two again, but add more shells to the enclosure before you return the aggressor. If the crab who wants a new shell has more empty shells to choose from, he is more likely to stop harassing other crabs.

Another way to discourage aggression among crabs is to provide them with more room. Giving them a bigger crabitat to roam through will help reduce incidences of territorial aggression.

Hermit crabs who persist in attacking other crabs for no apparent reason, or regardless of the number of vacant shells in the enclosure, should be permanently separated from the group. You may have to start another crabitat to keep the offending crab away from the crabs he is harassing. Since even aggressive crabs shouldn't live alone, be sure to give him a friend or two who are his size or bigger, to discourage further aggression.

Some crabs make a chirping sound when they are picked up.

Crab Sounds

Long-time hermit crab owners are familiar with a sound made by crabs when they are picked up or when they get into altercations with other crabs. Known as chirping by pet owners, and more technically referred to as *stridulation* by biologists, this vocalization sounds like an odd combination of noises, including a frog's croak and a cricket's chirp.

Scientists believe stridulation is created when a hermit crab rubs certain parts of his body together. You won't see your crab doing this (this vocalization is so mysterious, scientists are not completely sure how it happens), but you will hear the resulting sound.

Another sound familiar to crab owners is the clicking made when hermit crabs knock their shells together. Unlike stridulation, these clicking sounds are made inadvertently and usually happen when crabs are gathering in a food dish, climbing up a decoration en masse, or basically doing anything that brings them in close proximity to each other.

Make sure your crabs have plenty of roomy hiding spots so they can feel safe.

Hiding

In the wild, hermit crabs hide as a way to avoid predators. Hiding helps a hermit crab feel secure and reduces the animal's stress level. Hermit crabs have two ways of hiding: in their shells and in an external hiding place.

Because they carry their shells around with them, hermit crabs can easily hide at a moment's notice if they feel threatened. They withdraw as deeply into their shells as possible, covering the shell entrance with their large pincher to block off the opening from an intruder. (Hermit crabs who are living in shells that are too small will have trouble fitting all the way into the shell when they retreat.)

In nature, hermit crabs take hiding one step further by finding places they can hide in while they are retreating into their shells for sleep. This can be a pile of leaves, a coconut shell, a clump of rocks, or anything they can find that seems to provide security.

To help pet hermit crabs feel secure and stress-free, it's important to provide hiding places in their enclosure. Commercial reptile hiding places work great for hermit crabs, as do half-buried terra cotta pots and the bottoms of 1-liter plastic soda bottles.

If you provide your crabs with roomy hiding spots, you'll likely see them gathering together to sleep inside one of these protective covers.

Shell Swapping

One of the most amusing of hermit crab behaviors is the phenomenon of shell swapping. This is when one hermit crab abandons his shell in favor of another one, causing a chain reaction of shell changes that races through the crab population.

If you are lucky, you'll see this amusing game of musical shells take place. If you happen to see one of your crabs changing shells, pay attention. All the other crabs in the enclosure might start switching, too.

Chapter 10

Having Fun with Your Hermit Crabs

In addition to observing the antics of your hermit crabs and learning firsthand about the ocean creatures who live in your home, you can interact with your crabs in a number of ways to maximize your enjoyment of these interesting pets. As you interact with your crabs, though, it's important to remember that they are wild animals and will not immediately feel comfortable and relaxed in your home.

Handling

Before you do anything with your hermit crabs, it's important that you know how to handle these once-wild creatures. Hermit crabs can learn to enjoy being handled if you treat them with care and respect. It may take awhile for your crabs to become tame enough to enjoy handling. Start out slowly and wait until your crabs are comfortable with you putting your hand in their crabitat to feed them and clean up. When they stop retreating into their shells at the sight or touch of your hand on their shell or body, you can try handling them.

Crab Safety

Before picking up a crab, wash your hands with unscented soap and warm water to make sure you have gotten rid of any perfume or other residue that might bother your crabs.

When you handle one of your crabs for the first time, sit down to reduce the likelihood of your crab falling from up high. Crabs can easily toddle right off your hand and onto the floor, severely injuring themselves.

To hold your crab, flatten one hand, close your fingers together, and grasp your crab's shell with your other hand. Place the crab onto your flattened hand, taking care not to hold her by her shell for too long, since this will not only frighten her, but make it hard for her to stay inside her shell.

Your crab will probably hide in her shell when she feels herself being lifted, and will no doubt stay there for a long time. If you get tired of waiting for her to come out of her shell, you can put her back in her crabitat and try again later or the next day. Eventually, your crab will peek out of her shell and will come to learn that being held is not a bad thing. In time, she should start crawling around on your hand.

Watch for Pinching

If your crab pinches you when you are holding her, she probably feels insecure. Hermit crabs typically pinch when they are afraid and when they are worried that they will fall. (They pinch and hold on in an attempt to keep from falling.)

If your crab pinches you and you think she's afraid of falling, adjust your hand so that her body position is more secure, or lay your open hand on the floor of the crabitat and allow your crab to crawl off.

Pick up your crab by holding only her shell, then place her on your flat hand.

Your crab may be pinching you out of self-defense because she hasn't come to trust you yet. Avoid the urge to pull her off your hand, since this will only encourage her to hold on tighter. Try to simply lay your hand down in the crabitat and let her crawl off. If she won't let go, run your hand under warm water until she releases her grip.

Be patient with your crab and keep handling sessions short. In time, she'll learn that you aren't going to hurt her.

Crab Bonding

Once your crab is secure with the idea of being held, you can invite her to crawl onto your hand instead of having to pick her up by her shell.

Place a flat hand on the floor of the crabitat and wait for your crab to crawl onto it. She will most likely explore your hand with her antennae, and you'll enjoy the sensation of having her walking on your skin.

It's important to remember that trust is crucial when handling your hermit crab. Treat her gently and with respect and your crab will come to know you and gladly crawl onto your hand for a visit.

Hermit crab owners say they enjoy the tickly sensation of the crab walking on their hands.

Hand Feeding

Some hermit crab owners are able to teach their pets to eat from their hand. This takes time and patience, but is very rewarding when your crab comes to trust you enough to eat while you hold her.

Start out by getting your crab comfortable with being held. This may take some time, since you'll need to build trust. Once you get to the point where your crab feels safe when you are handling her (you'll know because she is out of her shell and exploring), you can try hand feeding.

If you already know what foods your crab likes best, grab a piece of her favorite food with your free hand, and hold the food up to the crab near her mouth and claws. If your crab is hungry and likes what you are offering, she just may take it from you and start eating.

Keep in mind that if your crab is not in the mood to eat, she won't take the food from you. Offering her food from your hand in the evening will encourage her to eat, since crabs do most of their eating at night.

Playtime

Many hermit crab owners take their crabs out of their crabitats every day and give the crabs a chance to explore other areas of the house, under supervision of course.

Safety First

If you like the idea of giving your hermit crabs some exercise and watching them explore, you'll need to take some precautions first. Make sure the temperature in your home is on the warm side before you take your crabs out of the comfort of their enclosure. The dead of winter is not usually a good time to let your crabs run loose. If you live in a warm, humid climate and your house is not air-conditioned, your crabs will enjoy the temperature.

Before letting your crabs loose on the floor of a room, "crab proof" the area to make sure they can't get into trouble. Watch out for areas where they could hide (and not be found), things they could climb on and tip over, and hazardous chemicals they could get into.

Hermit crabs and carpeting don't mix because the crabs' legs will catch on the carpet fiber. It's a good idea to put playing crabs in a room with solid flooring, or else cover a carpeted floor with a bedsheet.

Last but not least, make sure your crabs are protected from other pets, such as cats, dogs, and birds. One of your other animals may regard your toddling crab as prey and do irreparable harm to your little pet.

A Fun Environment

To encourage your hermit crabs to play when they are out of their crabitat, create an environment for them that will stimulate activity. You can do this by adding interesting items to the area where they are running loose. Here are some suggestions of objects that can be fun for crabs to play with, on, and around:

- Driftwood for climbing
- Rocks for climbing

Crab Racing

Hermit crab racing has become a popular form of entertainment at bars and restaurants in certain resort areas where hermit crabs are native—much to the dismay of many hermit crab lovers, who believe these races are very stressful for the crabs.

Public hermit crab races involve choosing a crab from a bucket, betting on her, and then seeing if she wins a race against a number of other crabs. Crabs are placed inside a circle, and the crab who gets to the outside of the circle first is the winner. The stress comes in when the crabs are put into and pulled out of the buckets, placed on a table, and exposed to cheering crowds. Some crabs reportedly fall off the table and are injured in some of these races.

The basics of crab racing can be enjoyed without stress to the crabs if you do it at home, with your own pets. If you set up the "racetrack" in an area of your home where your crabs are used to playing and create the circle on the floor rather than on a table top, your crabs can race one another stress-free.

Use a bedsheet as the floor of your racetrack and mark your circle with masking tape. Place all your crabs in the center of the circle and watch them as they scamper outward. You can bet with your friends and family, and award prizes to whoever picks the winning crab.

- Empty toilet paper rolls for investigating (only if your crabs are small enough not to get stuck inside them)
- A small stack of bricks for climbing
- Cardboard boxes for investigating
- A vertical cat scratching post for climbing (but avoid the ones that are wrapped in carpeting)

Another option for hermit crab playtime is a hamster play ball. Your hermit crab can be placed inside this transparent plastic ball (available at pet supply stores) and allowed to wander all around the house from inside the safety of the ball.

Whenever your crabs are playing, supervise them to make sure they don't get into trouble. If you can't keep a close watch on them, put them back in their crabitat where you know they are safe.

Traveling with Your Crabs

Everyone takes vacations, even hermit crab owners! If you are going somewhere, you'll probably want to leave your hermit crabs at home in the safety of their crabitat, with a friend, neighbor, or professional pet sitter checking on them daily to give them food and water.

If you plan to play with your crabs outside of the crabitat, make sure their play area is interesting and safe.

Sometimes, however, you'll need to transport your hermit crabs. If you are moving to a new home or need to get out of your house in an emergency (a fire, hurricane, flood, or other disaster), your hermit crabs will need to go with you. Or maybe you are going on an extended visit somewhere and want to have your crabs with you.

In many cases, it will be difficult or impossible to transport your crabs' entire enclosure. Filled with substrate and decorations, the crabitat can be heavy and unwieldy. For this reason, you should always keep a travel home available for your crabs just in case they need to be away from home.

Transport Container

If you are moving or have an emergency where you have to take your crabs away from home, a small carrier can do the job. Available at pet supply stores, these plastic containers are often sold to use with small mammals, such as mice and hamsters. Some are sold as permanent

---

T I P

Finding a Pet Sitter

To find an experienced, professional pet sitter in your area, check out the Web sites of Pet Sitters International (www.petsit.com) and the National Association of Professional Pet Sitters (www.petsitters.org).

crab habitats. Although they are too small and not well insulated enough to be used as a permanent home for hermit crabs, they can be very handy as travel carriers for hermit crabs.

If you plan to use one of these containers to travel with your hermit crabs, keep in mind that you will need to provide some of the necessities of home. Place some of the same substrate your crabs are used to in the container, and provide a secure hiding place that won't slip or tip. Food and water dishes are also important, as well as a natural sponge and dechlorinating and saline solutions for the crabs' water. Bring some of your crabs' commercial crab food, and plan on giving them fresh fruit and vegetables for meals as well.

It's best to only travel with your hermit crabs during warm weather, since these creatures need to stay in temperatures of about 76 to 82 degrees Fahrenheit. If you have to move them in their transport container during the winter or when it's cool out, you'll need to do everything you can to keep them warm. Keep the travel carrier out of the cold and wind, and place it in the warmest area of your car or wherever you are staying. (Do not put the carrier next to a heater, however, since this will dry out your crabs!)

Humidity is also important to hermit crabs who are traveling. Bring a mister with you to spray the inside of the travel carrier several times a day with

Humidity is important to crabs at home and on the go. Don't forget to mist your crabs regularly, no matter where you are.

dechlorinated water to keep the area moist. Keep parts of the substrate moist and use a cover to keep moisture inside the carrier.

Temporary Home

If you plan on being away from home for more than just a few days, you should set up a temporary home for your crabs. This should be a small aquarium (the 2-gallon type sold for fish will work), and should have a cover. Because hermit crabs need heat to stay alive, you'll need a heat source such as an undertank heating pad. Since most heating elements require electricity, you'll need somewhere you can plug this in once you arrive at your destination.

Your temporary hermit crab enclosure should also include the following:

- **Substrate.** Use the same substrate your hermit crab is used to having in her permanent crabitat.
- **Thermometer.** You'll need to make sure the temperature inside the tank stays between 76 and 82 degrees Fahrenheit. A thermometer will help you maintain the right air temperature.
- **Mister.** You'll need to spray your crabs' temporary home once to several times a day with dechlorinated water, depending on how dry the outside air is.
- **Natural sponge.** Keeping a natural sponge in your crabs' temporary home will help keep the humidity levels up.
- **Food and water dishes.** Shallow food and water dishes will enable you to feed and water your crabs as you would at home. Be sure to bring two water dishes—one for fresh water and the other for salt water.
- **Water treatments.** Don't forget to pack a product that will dechlorinate your hermit crabs' drinking water, as well as a solution that will salinate the other dish of water. If you plan to be away for awhile, your crabs need both fresh and salt water to stay healthy.
- **Hiding place.** Since this is just a temporary home for your crabs, you don't need to go crazy with decorations in the tank. However, it's a good idea to equip the temporary home with a hiding place or two to help the crabs feel secure. This is especially important because they will be taken out of their usual environment. Crabs can see what's going on outside their crabitat, and may be stressed by all the movement and new sights on the outside.
- **Food.** Don't forget to bring some of your crabs' commercial crab food, because this contains vitamins and minerals they need to stay healthy. If you won't have access to fresh fruits and vegetables, bring along a few of these as well, so you can offer them to your crabs in the evening.

Meeting Other Crab Owners

Something about hermit crabs makes people fall in love with these little creatures. The owners of hermit crabs love to talk about their pets and what they enjoy about them.

The Internet

Through the Internet, you can meet other hermit crab owners all around the world. Talking to other crab owners is a great way to learn more about how to care for your hermit crabs. You can read articles written by other crab owners and ask questions to find out more about your crabs' care and behavior.

There are a number of excellent hermit crab Web sites. Some of these sites have message boards, which enable users to post questions and have discussions with other crab owners. You can find a list of hermit crab Web sites in the appendix.

You may want to share with others the fun you have with your hermit crabs.

Four-H Clubs

Four-H, which is short for Head, Heart, Hands, and Health, began in the early part of the twentieth century with a community of farmers who wanted to encourage the development of agrarian skills in children. In 1907, it officially became part of the United States Department of Agriculture (USDA).

Since then, the 4-H youth program has grown into a large national network of local clubs, featuring projects that range from computers to cattle. Some groups have a hermit crab project or other pet projects that include caring for reptiles and other small pets like hermit crabs. Four-H is an excellent way for young hermit crab owners to learn all about caring for these creatures.

Open to children ages 9 to 19 (and sometimes younger, depending on the individual club), 4-H pet projects feature hands-on learning. Children are taught how to feed, care for, and handle their small pets.

To obtain information on a local 4-H hermit crab project, contact your county extension office by looking in your telephone directory. For general information about 4-H, contact the National 4-H Council listed in the appendix.

Hermit Crab Conventions

In 2000, ten hermit crab owners gathered at Christa Wilkin's house to share their love of these fascinating pets. This gathering served as the Hermit Crab Association's first convention. In recent years, the size and scope of HCA conventions have grown. In 2004, the convention was held in Key West, Florida. Crab lovers participated in a number of social activities, including kayaking, snorkeling, and an educational trip to a local reef. Educational information was a part of the convention as well, and information sheets on hermit crab care were provided. A second convention, sponsored by the Hermit Crab Association (HCA), was held in 2005 in Galveston, Texas.

Another HCA-sponsored hermit crab convention may take place in the near future. Attending one of these events is not only fun, but can provide a wealth of knowledge on how to care for and enjoy your hermit crabs. If you're interested in attending a convention, check out the HCA Web site (www.hermit crabassociation.com) for information.

Learning More About
Your Hermit Crabs

Some Good Books

Burggren, Warren W., *Biology of the Land Crabs,* Cambridge University Press, 1988.

De Vosjoli, Philippe, *The Care of Land Hermit Crabs,* Advanced Vivarium Systems, 1999.

Fox, Sue, *Hermit Crabs: A Complete Pet Owner's Manual,* Barron's Educational Series, 2000.

Ingle, R.W., *Crayfishes, Lobsters and Crabs of Europe: An Illustrated Guide to Common and Traded Species,* Cambridge University Press, 1997.

Johnson, Sylvia, *Hermit Crabs,* Lerner Publications, 1989.

Pohl, Kathleen, *Hermit Crabs,* Raintree Publishers, 1986.

Ruppert, Edward E., and Richard S. Fox, *Seashore Animals of the Southeast: A Guide to Common Shallow-Water Invertebrates of the Southeast,* University of Southern Carolina Press, 1988.

Children's Fiction

Boyce, Katie, *Hector the Hermit Crab,* Bloomsbury USA Children's Books, 2003.

Carle, Eric, *A House for Hermit Crab,* Picture Book Studio, 1991.

Glaser, Michael, *Does Anyone Know Where a Hermit Crab Goes?,* Knickerbocker Publishing Co., 1983.

McGee, Caroline C., *Matt the Moody Hermit Crab,* Soulwave Publishing, 2002.

Peet, Bill, *Kermit the Hermit,* Houghton Mifflin, 1965.

Weathers, Andrea, *Hermy the Hermit Crab Goes Shopping,* Legacy Publications, 2001.

Education

National 4-H Council
7100 Connecticut Ave.
Chevy Chase, MD 20815
(301) 961-2800
www.4husa.org

Online Resources

Crab Information

Crabby Talk

www.crabbytalk.com

The hermit crab species identification feature takes you around the world with hermit crabs. Article archives include information on care, diet, and crabitats. There is also advice about buying your first hermit crab. Places to shop, big photos, and daily exploits of hermies round out this site.

The Crab Street Journal

www.crabstreetjournal.org

An online magazine devoted to hermit crabs and their owners. This is a very comprehensive site, and includes downloadable care sheets, information about crabs available for adoption, a section for kids, maps that show the distribution of hermit crabs around the world, products to buy, and ideas for the ideal crabitat.

Epicurean Hermit

www.epicureanhermit.com

This Web site is devoted to nutrition and recipes for hermit crabs. It features articles related to hermit crab diet, news and products about the hermit crab diet, and recipes to tempt even the fussiest of hermit crabs.

Hermit-Crabs.com
www.hermit-crabs.com
This site is run by Christa Wilkin, who hosted the first hermit crab convention in 2000. It covers hermit crab care and behavior, including a lot of information on the molt, and esoteric subjects such as sexing your hermit crabs and dealing with aggression. A typical day in the life of a hermit crab is nicely described.

Hermit Crab Association
www.hermitcrabassociation.com
The Hermit Crab Association is an online community of land hermit crab lovers from around the world. It includes care and adoption information, and lively chatrooms and user groups.

Hermit Crab Paradise
www.hermitcrabparadise.com
This is a Web site for hermit crabs and their owners. Features include a photo gallery and care information.

Hug a Lil' Crab
hugalilcrab.com
Big, fun photos are featured on this site. There is also a shopping page and owner forums, plus a diary of a typical hermit crab's life.

I Have Crabs
www.ihavecrabs.com
A care information and forum for hermit crab owners. Includes a tech page to teach owners how to create special crabitat features, such as a lamp that simulates moonlight.

Mrs. Poppy Puff
www.mrspoppypuff.com
A site for hermit crab lovers. This is an owner's site and features photos, video, and information about the owner's pet hermit crabs.

Hermit Crab Product Suppliers

Dr. Jungle's Animal World
animal-world.com

Care-a-Lot Pet Supply
www.carealotpets.com

Crab Island
www.reptiledepot.com/hermit.html

Florida Marine Research
www.fmrpets.com

Hermit Crabs R Us
www.thehcrustore.com

Hermit Supply
www.hermitsupply.com

Naples Sea Shell Company
www.naplesseashellcompany.com/hermit_crab_shells.htm

Paradise Pet Supply
www.hermits-direct.net/menu_livehermits

Petco
www.petco.com

Pet Discounters
www.petdiscounters.com

Petsmart
www.petsmart.com

Pets Warehouse
www.pets-warehouse.com

Reptile Direct
www.reptiledirect.com

Sea Shell City
www.seashellcity.com

Seashells.com
seashells.com/hermitcrabs/hermitcrabhuts.htm

Sea-Shells.net
www.sea-shells.net

Summit Pet Product Distributors
www.summitpet.com

The Crabby Shack
www.crabbyshack.com

Zoo Med Laboratories
www.zoomed.com

Index

abdomen, 12, 15

activity level, health indicator, 41–42

adoptions, 39

age, selection, 42–43

aggression, behavior traits, 102

anatomy, illustrated, 12

animal shelters, adoption resource, 39

antennae, 12, 15

 health indicator, 42

 illness indicator, 81

 socialization behavior, 98

appendages, regrowth, 15, 85

appetite increase, molting sign, 91

aquarium gravel, 48–49

aquatic hermit crabs, saltwater aquariums, 20

Arthropoda phylum, 13–16

attention, ownership, 29–31

bark

 dietary guidelines, 66–67

 substrate pros/cons, 49

baths, humidity, 83

behavior traits

 aggression, 102

 climbing, 100–101

 digging, 101–102

 eating, 99

 hiding, 104–105

 nocturnal animals, 99

 self-grooming, 99–100

 shell swapping, 105

 socialization, 98

 vocalizations, 103

bonding, owner/crab interaction, 108

breeding, salt water requirement, 17–18

buying hermit crabs, 37–39

calcium, food sources, 67

Caribbean hermit crab *(Coenobita com-pressus)*, saltwater guidelines, 71

Caribbean land crab *(Coenobita clypeatus)*, 18–19, 40, 74

celebrity crabs, 25

children, hermit crab interaction, 34–36

children's books, 25

chilling, heat maintenance, 82

chirping, communication, 17, 103

chores, daily/monthly care, 34

claws, 12, 15

clicking sounds, communication, 103

climbing

 behavior traits, 100–101

 playtime guidelines, 109–110

climbing sticks, 55

coconut/robber hermit crab *(Coenobitidae birgus latro)*, 22

Coenobita compressus, shell preferences, 74

commercial foods, 61–62

concave/red hermit crab *(Coenobita cavipes)*, 21

crabitat

 climbing mats/sticks, 55

 decorations, 57

 extra shells, 56–57

 food bowls, 54

 fresh water/salt water, 70–71

 full-spectrum lighting fixtures, 53

 heat (temperature) guidelines, 82

 heat sources, 49–51

crabitat *(cont.)*
    hiding places (shelters), 54–55
    humidity gauge, 81–82
    humidity sources, 51–53
    hygiene importance, 89
    isolation tanks, 57, 59
    location, 58
    mite infestations, 85–87
    molted crab return guidelines, 95
    molting tanks, 93–95
    newcomer acclimation, 59
    playtime environment, 109–111
    shopping list, 52
    substrates, 48–49
    tank guidelines, 46–47
    travel carriers, 111–113
    water conditioners, 56
    water dishes, 53–54
crab racing, 110
crustaceans, 14–15, 23–24
cuddle factor, ownership, 32–34
cuttlebones, calcium source, 67

daily care, 29–31, 34
dairy products, avoiding, 66
decorations, 57
dehydration, 81–82
diet, 89
digging, 91, 101–102

eating, 99
Ecuadorian hermit crab *(Coenobita compressus)*, 19–20, 40
environment
    crabitat location guidelines, 58
    habitat concerns, 25–27
    playtime guidelines, 109–111
equipment/supplies, shopping list, 52
exoskeleton, molting process, 14, 91–95
eyes, 12, 15

females, 17–18, 41
fighting, shell, 78, 79, 102
financial commitment, ownership, 30
fish/turtle foods, diet guidelines, 65–66

foam board, tank insulation, 50–51
food bowls, 54, 94, 113
food refusal, illness indicator, 81
foods
    calcium sources, 67
    commercial, 61–62
    dairy products, 66
    fish/turtle, 65–66
    fruits, 63, 64–65
    hand feeding, 108–109
    herbs, 63, 64
    insects, 66–67
    leaves/bark, 66
    malnutrition indicators, 83–84
    molted exoskeletons, 95
    people foods, 66
    protein sources, 65
    purchasing guidelines, 55–56
    recipes, 68
    serving guidelines, 69–70
    travel carriers, 113
    vegetables, 62–63, 64
4-H clubs, meeting others, 114–115
Fruit and Nut Salad recipe, 68
fruit, dietary guidelines, 63, 64–65
full-spectrum lighting fixtures, 53

gastropods, shell source, 16
gel limbs, molting sign, 92
gender, 41
genopores, 41
gills, 12, 15
goldfish bowls, inadequate homes, 47
gray/white hermit crab *(Coenobita rugosus)*, 22

habitat. *See also* crabitat
    environmental concerns, 25–27
    health indicator, 42
hamster balls, playtime uses, 110–111
hand feeding, 108–109
handling, 106–108
health problems
    chilling, 82
    dehydration, 81–82

lost limbs, 84–85
malnutrition, 83–84
mites, 85–87
molting, 91–95
out of the shell, reasons, 89–90
shell disease, 87–88
heat (temperature)
chilling, 82
crabitat guidelines, 49–51, 82
health importance, 88–89
heat lamps, 50
heat rocks, 50
heat sources, molting tanks, 93
herbs, dietary guidelines, 63, 64
Hermit Crab Association (HCA), 115
hermit crab conventions, 115
hiding behavior, 104–105
hiding places (shelters), 94, 113
household products, health risks, 89
households
crabitat location guidelines, 58
terrarium space requirements, 30
human garbage, shell source, 16
humidity
bath, 83
care, 31
dehydration concerns, 81–82
habitat sources, 51–53
health importance, 88
humidity gauge, 53, 81–82

Indonesian hermit crab (Coenobita
brevimanus), 20–21
insects, dietary guidelines, 66–67
insulation, foam board, 50–51
Internet, meeting other owners, 114
Internet sellers, 38
intertidal hermit crab, 20
isolation tank, 59, 93–95

larvae, breeding process, 17–18
leaves, dietary guidelines, 66–67
legs, 12, 15
lethargy, molting sign, 92

lighting fixtures, full-spectrum, 53
limbs, 81, 84–85, 92

males, 17–18, 41
malnutrition, illness indicator, 83–84
mats, climbing, 55
misters, 53, 113
mites, 85–87
molting
crabitat return guidelines, 95
dead/near dead appearance, 92
exoskeleton shedding process, 14
isolation tanks, 93–95
mid-molt indicators, 93
preparation signs, 91–92
monthly care, chores, 34
mouth, 12, 15
mulch, substrate pros/cons, 49
mythology, hermit crabs, 24

National Association of Professional Pet
Sitters, 111
natural habitat, 25–27
natural sea sponges, 53, 113
nocturnal animals, 99

ownership
children's responsibilities, 34–36
cuddle factor, 32–34
daily care chores, 34
meeting other owners, 114–115
monthly care chores, 34
reasons for, 28–29
responsibilities, 29–32

painted shells, 76–77
parasites, 42, 85–87
people foods, dietary guidelines, 66
pericardial sac, molting sign, 92
pets (other), predatory concerns, 31, 60
pet sitters, 111
pet stores, 37–38
physical health, desirable traits, 40–42
playtime, 109–111

pollution, 27
protein, food sources, 65

recipes, 68
red/concave hermit crab (Coenobita cavipes), 21
reproductive organs, 41
rescue groups, 39
robber/coconut hermit crab (Coenobitidae birgus latro), 22

salt water, 70–71
saltwater aquariums, 20
sand, substrate, 48
scientific classification, 13–16
sea sponges, 53, 113
seawater, 70–71
self-grooming, 99–100
shell disease, 87–88
shell leaving, 89–90
shells
    acquiring, 16
    cleaning activities, 99–100
    cleaning process, 77
    crabitat accessory, 56–57
    entering techniques, 75
    environmental concerns, 25–27
    fights, 78, 79
    growth factors, 72–73
    interior remodeling process, 74–75
    moisture requirements, 79
    paint, 76–77
    purchasing, 76
    selection process, 73–74
    species preferences, 74
    varieties, 75
shell swapping, 105
shelters, 54–55, 94, 113
Shrimp and Egg Feast recipe, 68
size, selection element, 42–43
sluggishness, 81
socialization
    behavior traits, 98
    breeding process, 17–18
    meeting other owners, 114–115

multiple pet benefits, 39
vocal communications, 17
sticks, climbing, 55
strawberry hermit crab (Coenobita perlatus), 21
stress, prevention, 89
stridulation, chirping sounds, 17, 103
substrates
    mite infestations, 85–87
    molting tanks, 93
    purchasing, 48–49
    travel carriers, 113
supplies/equipment, shopping list, 52

table salt, avoiding, 70
tankmates, 20, 78, 79
tanks. See crabitat
temperature (heat)
    care consideration, 31
    chilling, 82
    crabitat guidelines, 49–51, 82
    health, 88–89
terrariums. See crabitat
thermometers, 50, 51, 113
tide pools, 20
travel carriers, 57, 111–113
tree bark/leaves, diet, 66–67
Tuna and Veggie Casserole recipe, 68
turtle/fish foods, diet, 65–66

undertank heaters, 50

vacations, travel guidelines, 111–113
vegetables, dietary guidelines, 62–63, 64
vocalizations, 17, 103

water, 70–71, 79, 89
water conditioners, 56
water dishes, 52–54, 93, 113
water intake, molting sign, 91, 92
weight, health indicator, 42
West Atlantic hermit crab (Coenobita clypeatus), 18–19, 40
white/gray hermit crab (Coenobita rugosus), 22

Photo Credits:

Isabelle Francais: 10–11, 14, 19, 25, 28, 32, 37, 49, 58, 62, 67, 77, 84, 90, 96–97, 103, 107, 111, 114

Teresa Lenihan: 3, 6–7, 13, 17, 21, 23, 26, 30, 34, 35, 38, 40, 42, 44–45, 46, 47, 51, 54, 55, 56, 57, 61, 63, 69, 70, 72, 73, 74, 78, 79, 80, 82, 86, 87, 91, 94, 98, 100, 101, 104, 106, 108, 112, 126, 127, 128

Notes

Notes

Notes